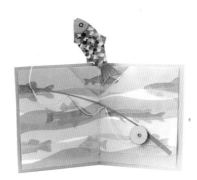

Paper Pop Up

Dorothy Wood

David and Charles

A DAVID & CHARLES BOOK
Copyright © David & Charles Limited 2007

David & Charles is an F+W Publications Inc. company
4700 East Galbraith Road
Cincinnati, OH 45236

First published in 2007

Text and project designs copyright © Dorothy Wood 2007

Dorothy Wood has asserted her right to be identified as author of this
work in accordance with the Copyright, Designs and Patents Act, 1988.

A catalogue record for this book is available from the British Library.

ISBN-13: 978-0-7153-2590-2 (hardback)
ISBN-10: 0-7153-2590-6 (hardback)
ISBN-13: 978-0-7153-2430-1 (paperback)
ISBN-10: 0-7153-2430-6 (paperback)

Printed in China by SNP Leefung
for David & Charles
Brunel House   Newton Abbot   Devon

Executive Editor Cheryl Brown
Editor Jennifer Proverbs
Desk Editor Bethany Dymond
Art Editor Prudence Rogers
Designer Tracey Woodward
Production Controller Ros Napper
Project Editor Jo Richardson
Photographer Simon Whitmore

Visit our website at www.davidandcharles.co.uk

David & Charles books are available from all good bookshops;
alternatively you can contact our Orderline on 0870 9908222 or write
to us at FREEPOST EX2 110, D&C Direct, Newton Abbot, TQ12 4ZZ
(no stamp required UK only); US customers call 800-289-0963 and
Canadian customers call 800-840-5220.

Contents

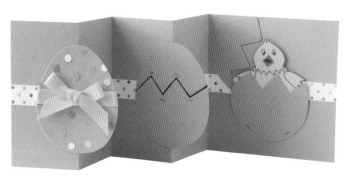

Conceal… Reveal… Pop-up Appeal!

Pop-up cards are quite magical because of the surprise and delight that comes when you open, pull or operate the pop-up element. It's one of the simple things in life guaranteed to put a smile on the recipient's face – especially if it works faultlessly! This 'wow' factor is an essential aspect of pop-up papercrafting, and the challenge of this book was to devise a variety of projects that optimized the unexpected.

The result is a huge range of pop-up devices for you to try, each carefully designed and presented with clear instructions and templates so that you can make up the project items as quickly and easily as possible. Every chapter features an unusual card design with a different pop-up element, and most of the accompanying projects incorporate a unique built-in surprise component.

The projects are divided into ten chapters, each focusing on a key occasion when you would invariably send a card or mark it in some way. In addition to birthdays, anniversaries and other major milestones, there are the special seasonal celebrations throughout the year such as Easter, Halloween and Mother's Day, which are perfect for pop-up papercrafting – each so different in nature and therefore offering its own creative opportunities. The theme of each chapter lends itself to a particular colour palette as well as design ideas – a spell book to create a spooky mood on Halloween, a baby album to record those precious first days or a fun Easter box for filling up with a feast of eggs! Add to all this specially conceived papercrafting the inventive

pop-up or surprise elements, and the projects literally take on an extra dimension, being transformed from the static and two-dimensional into exciting interactive designs.

Pop-up papercrafting is easier than ever because there is such a wealth of papers and card available to help you create fantastic projects. Once restricted to primary colours, card now comes in a huge array of shades, and coordinating papers are available in every imaginable colour and pattern. Advances in adhesives and glue products have taken papercrafting to a new level of technical sophistication, and the popularity of scrapbooking and card making has encouraged craft outlets to stock a wide range of embellishments such as stickers, buttons, ribbons and charms to add the ideal finishing touches to any handcrafted item.

Remember that all the projects can be adapted for alternative occasions. The Card Gallery on pages 92–97 shows just how easy it is to use the pop-up techniques in a completely different way, so you can draw on these examples as inspiration for creating your own unique designs. In fact, there are so many great ideas to choose from, you'll find it hard to decide which one to try first!

Getting Started

Every project in this book requires some papercrafting tools and basic materials, and involve a few key techniques, so here is what you need to get you started.

Basic Tool Kit

The 'You Will Need' list for each project itemizes any specialist tools together with all the materials required to make the item, but it assumes that you have this basic tool kit.

Card, Board and Printable Film

Stock basic white card in a range of thicknesses: lightweight, medium and heavyweight card (see page 8). Stationery shops and suppliers sell grey board – an extra-thick card often with one white side ideal for album covers and other structural work. Self-adhesive clear printable film, e.g. Safmat™, is one of the easiest ways to add text or numbers to cards or scrapbook pages. You simply type what you need onto a computer and print out onto the film, using photo-print quality for the best results. As the film is clear, it is almost invisible in use.

Cutting Equipment

Keep a selection of craft knives and blades for different tasks. Change blades as soon as it becomes harder to cut and keep blunt blades in a tin box so that you can dispose of them safely. Although not essential, rotary cutters and paper trimmers take the hard work out of cutting card and papers. Trimmers are ideal for single sheets and rotary cutters can cut through several layers at one go. Trimmers are ideal for card making, as some have a scoring slider so that you can both cut and fold cards.

Basic Tools and Materials Checklist

* white paper and card (1)
* tracing paper (2)
* grey board (3)
* self-adhesive clear printable film, e.g. Safmat™
* bone folder (4)
* embossing tool (5)
* swivel-tip craft knife (6)
* scalpel (7)
* general-purpose craft knife (8)
* general-purpose craft scissors (9)
* small, pointed scissors (10)
* eraser (11)
* fine-line black pen (12)
* propelling pencil with 0.7mm lead (13)
* soft (B) pencil (14)
* Mod Podge™ (15)
* paintbrushes – one coarse-bristled for glue (16)
* dry adhesive sheets (17)
* PVA (white) glue (18)
* glue stick (19)
* strong glue
* adhesive foam pads
* double-sided tape (20)
* dry adhesive tape (21)
* craft glue dots (22)
* metal safety ruler (23)
* self-healing cutting mat (24)
* paper trimmer (25)
* paper pricker
* holepunches (26)
* eyelet setter (27)
* hammer (28)
* setting mat (29)

Adhesives

Put PVA (white) glue in a small plastic bottle and attach a metal nozzle for fine work. Use dry adhesive sheets and tape for a clean, professional finish to your card making, as well as craft glue dots for attaching embellishments. If you want to try some of the altered art projects, such as the Tiny Tot's Trinket Tin on page 17, matt Mod Podge™ is ideal and can be used as a varnish to protect the item. It is also available in gloss finish. Keep a separate paintbrush with coarse bristles for applying the glue and wash thoroughly after use. Adhesive foam pads are a quick and easy way of raising items to create a 3-D effect.

Holepunches, Eyelet Setter and Mat

Some holepunches require a hammer, but more recently developed styles have an in-built mechanism that does the same job. You will also need an eyelet setter, in conjunction with the holepunch and hammer, for fixing eyelets in place. Use a separate small mat for punching holes and setting eyelets to avoid damaging your cutting mat.

Working the Projects

These are the basic techniques and useful information you need to make the projects in the book.

What You Need to Know...

* Use the specified weight of card so that the project holds its shape and the pop-up mechanism works: lightweight is 160–180gsm, medium 200–230gsm and heavyweight 280–300gsm.

* If you don't have thick card, stick two pieces of thinner card back to back for added strength.

* Follow either the metric or imperial measurements and don't mix the two.

* Measurements are listed width first and then height.

Drawing

Keep your pencil sharp at all times for accurate marking or use a clutch or propelling pencil with a 0.7mm lead (thinner leads tend to break all the time). A soft lead (B) in one pencil is useful for transferring designs that you have copied onto tracing paper (see page 98).

Folding

To make folds look better and lie flat, first find the grain direction of your paper or card. Fold it in half and crease it with your finger, open out and then fold in half again the other way. The rough fold is perpendicular to the grain and the smooth fold is parallel to the grain. If you are still unsure, flex the paper or card widthways and then lengthways. The sheet will bend more easily into a tighter curve with the grain. Cut the card or paper for the project so that the main folds will lie in the same direction as the grain.

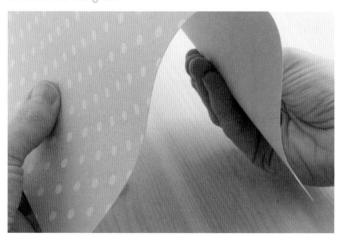

Cutting

Use scissors, craft knives or paper trimmers to cut paper and card. Be guided by the project instructions or photographs.

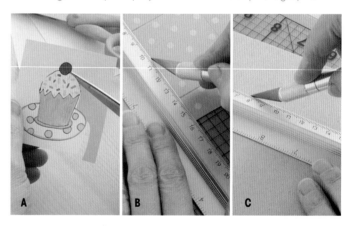

* Use larger scissors for basic paper cutting and small, pointed scissors for intricate cutting out. If you want to avoid the white core showing, hold the scissors at an angle to create a bevelled edge (A).

* A craft knife with a pointed blade is ideal for fine work. Use deeper blades for cutting against a metal safety ruler. Always cut with a craft knife on a self-healing cutting mat to make cutting easier and to protect the work surface.

* When using a craft knife, always cut with the section you want to use under the ruler so that if the knife slips it will cut into the waste section of the paper or card (B).

* Hold the craft knife at a 45-degree angle when cutting so that it cuts cleanly. Don't press too hard – with thicker card, cut through the top layer and then cut again (C).

Scoring

Use a ruler and embossing tool (or empty ballpoint pen) or a paper trimmer with a scoring slider for scoring. For valley folds, score the right side of the card or paper; for mountain folds, score the reverse side.

A valley fold is on the left-hand side and a mountain fold on the right.

1 Mark the card or paper lightly with a pencil at the top and bottom edges where you want to score or position the card against lines on the cutting mat. Line the ruler up with the marks, marginally to the left-hand side, and run an embossing tool down the ruler. Press lightly on paper and more firmly on card.

2 Fold the card or paper along the score line, then sharpen the crease with a bone folder. Although not shown for clarity, laying lightweight paper along the fold first prevents shiny marks. Pop-up mechanisms work more accurately and efficiently if the creases have been sharpened before assembly.

Finishing Pop-up Cards

The inside of a pop-up card is often so involved that it's easy to forget that the outside needs decorating too. Pop-up cards are bulkier than regular cards because there are usually several layers of folded card inside, so they don't fold completely flat and the surprise effect can be diminished if the card springs open when the recipient removes it from the envelope. Incorporating unusual closures as part of the outside card design is an ideal solution. Bear in mind the way the card opens depending on whether it is a portrait or landscape card.

* Cut a strip of card and fold around the card. Stick the ends together to create a removable band and decorate to suit the design.

* Stick a length of ribbon to the back of the card and wrap around the whole card before tying at the front.

* Add a flap to the back edge of the card. Attach a card disc to the flap and the main card, and secure by wrapping fine string around the two card discs.

* Cut one or two long tabs on the back panel of the card and two slits on the front panel for each tab. Tuck the tabs through the two slots to close.

* Attach a length of ribbon or cord at the edge of the card on the front and back and tie in a bow.

An Amazing Arrival

The arrival of a new baby is a momentous event that cries out to be celebrated in creative style. Match the mood of wonder and joy with these cutely crafted keepsake items, which offer a variety of clever ways of preserving those precious early days.

Add to the parents' delight and amazement with a card that features a pile of baby building blocks, which playfully pop out of a colourful background on opening. Once things have settled into a routine, new mums can take a little time out to go through all the heart-warming photos and create an album that captures the key moments of those wonderful first days. A child's board book from a charity shop provides an ideal base, which can be painted and embellished to suit a boy or a girl. Transform an ordinary tin box with a collage of baby-themed patterned papers to hold a gift for the new arrival, and wait for mum's enchanted reaction when she opens the box and a plethora of baby trinkets comes unexpectedly tumbling out.

Building for the Future The pop-up element of this card is ingeniously designed in graduated layers to make the stacked building blocks look very realistic.

Charmed Life Several pages of the board book are stuck together and a secret compartment cut out of the glued section to hold a more substantial memento.

Tiny Tot's Trinket Tin Cute baby embellishments attached to lengths of fine organza ribbon are threaded through the box lid. The lid can then be hung over the baby's cot as a mobile.

Building for the Future

YOU WILL NEED

* baby patterned papers – floral, striped
* pink card
* dual-tip pastel marker pens – pink, blue, yellow, green
* baby rubdown or vellum stickers
* embellishments – baby rattle, baby dress
* 46cm (18in) length of pink grosgrain ribbon
* Basic Tool Kit (see page 6)

1 Cut a 21 x 14.5cm (8¼ x 5¾in) piece of white medium card and score across the centre between the two long sides. Transfer the template, including all the inner details, on page 99 onto white lightweight card and cut out around the outside edge. Lay the template centrally on the card so the line marked A–B is level with the fold line. Draw around the outside edge with a pencil, then mark the inner details with a pin.

2 Draw in the remaining lines, drawing the blocks with very light pencil marks. Cut the vertical solid lines using a craft knife and metal safety ruler. Score the horizontal dashed lines. Rub out the pencil marks along the cut and scored lines.

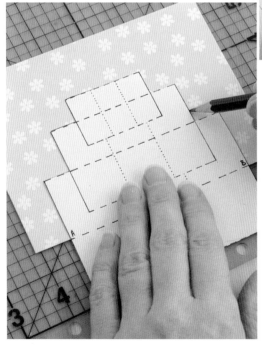

3 Colour the edges of the individual building blocks using dual-tip marker pens, colouring either side of the scored and dotted lines, making the top and side of each block the same colour. Use several pastel shades, so that no two adjacent blocks are the same colour. Make the coloured borders slightly narrower as the blocks get smaller.

4 Cut a 10.5 x 14.5cm (4⅛ x 5¾in) piece of floral patterned paper and striped patterned paper. Lay the template centrally on the floral patterned paper so that the line marked A–B is level with the bottom edge. Draw around the outside edge and cut along the line. Repeat with the striped patterned paper so that the A–B line is level with the top edge and cut along the line.

5 Push out the boxes on the card to create the pop-up effect. Close the card and crease all the folds firmly. Stick the striped patterned paper around the bottom of the building blocks for a carpet and use the floral patterned paper as a wallpaper background.

6 Decorate the building blocks with baby rubdown or vellum stickers. Attach a baby rattle embellishment on the 'carpet' in front of the blocks.

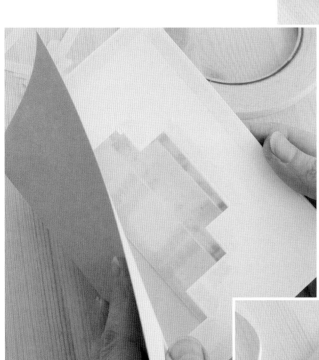

7 Cut a piece of pink card 21 x 14.5cm (8¼ x 5¾in), score widthways down the centre and fold in half. Close the pop-up card. Place strips of double-sided tape along the bottom and sides of the front and back of the pop-up card. Remove the backing paper on one side first and stick onto the pink card, then repeat with the second side.

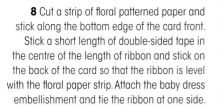

8 Cut a strip of floral patterned paper and stick along the bottom edge of the card front. Stick a short length of double-sided tape in the centre of the length of ribbon and stick on the back of the card so that the ribbon is level with the floral paper strip. Attach the baby dress embellishment and tie the ribbon at one side.

BRIGHT IDEA
Use double-sided tape or a dry adhesive sheet to stick the patterned papers to the card so that the paper doesn't buckle.

Charmed Life

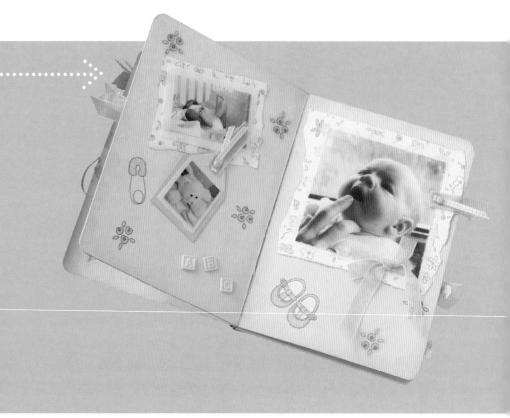

YOU WILL NEED

- child's board book
- parchment paper
- pink baby patterned papers
- acetate
- white acrylic gesso
- pink and white acrylic paint
- inkpads – several shades of pink
- colouring pens or pencils
- baby photos
- pink rickrack braid
- pink sheer and gingham ribbon
- letter rubdown or vellum stickers
- baby stickers and embellishments
- fine sandpaper
- sponge dauber or cosmetic sponge
- border punch
- pink sewing thread and sewing machine
- envelope template
- pastel-coloured paper fastener (brad)
- scallop-edged scissors
- Dimensional Magic™
- Basic Tool Kit (see page 6)

1 Prepare the board book ready to paint in one of two ways: you can either sand the pages to remove the shiny surface or simply peel off the top layer of shiny paper. This last method is ideal, as it removes some of the bulk, before you add it again with paint and paper embellishment! You may need to lightly sand the pages to remove any rough edges.

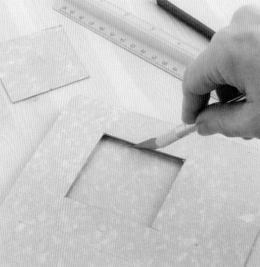

2 To make a secret compartment for a gift or memento such as a bracelet or lock of hair, decide how many pages you need to achieve the depth of hole required. Mark a 6cm (2⅜in) square (or other size) on the first of the pages, say six or seven from the back of the book, and cut along the lines using a craft knife and metal safety ruler. Cut through the underlying layers, one at a time, being guided by the faint marks from the previous cut. Stop before you cut through the back page. Stick the pages together using strong glue. Brush the glue close to the edge of the apertures and the side edges so that there are no gaps. Leave under a heavy weight until completely dry.

BRIGHT IDEA
The number of pages needed for the compartment depends on their thickness. Begin near the back and cut more if required.

3 Paint the entire book, inside and out, with a thin coat of white acrylic gesso. Stand it up to dry, with the pages sitting open, away from direct heat. Once dry, mix the pink and white paint to a pale shade of pink and paint the pages, again leaving it standing up to dry.

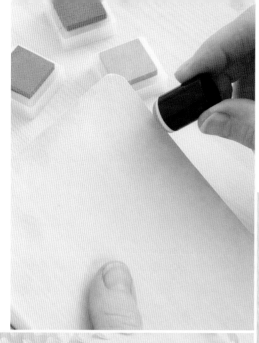

4 Using several different shades of pink ink and a sponge dauber or cosmetic sponge, dab colour all over the book, applying darker pink around the edges of the pages. Leave to dry as in Step 3.

BRIGHT IDEA
Once the board book has dried, if the pages have buckled slightly, leave under a heavy weight overnight to flatten.

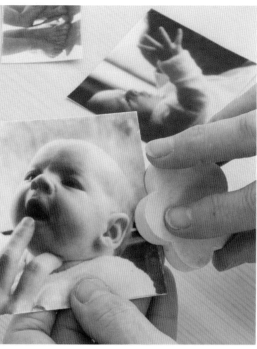

5 Choose a few photos that you would like to feature in your album and then trim to size, or use a software program on a computer to reduce or enlarge sections that you like and then print them out onto glossy photographic paper using a colour printer. Photos tend to look better in altered albums if you sand the edges with fine sandpaper.

6 To make a lacy border, cut a 5cm (2in) wide strip of parchment paper. Mark the centre, then working outwards from this, use a border punch to create the lace pattern down one side. Turn the paper around and punch down the other side. Lay a piece of pink rickrack braid down the centre and machine stitch.

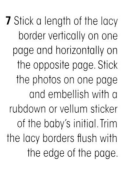

7 Stick a length of the lacy border vertically on one page and horizontally on the opposite page. Stick the photos on one page and embellish with a rubdown or vellum sticker of the baby's initial. Trim the lacy borders flush with the edge of the page.

8 Make a parchment envelope for an item of memorabilia for the opposite page, using an envelope template and extending the shape as required until it is long enough to hold the item, e.g. the hospital wristband. Embellish the envelope with ribbon and rickrack braid, held in place with a paper fastener (brad) and a real photo sticker.

BRIGHT IDEA
Embellish the pages with rickrack braid, metal baby charms and pastel buttons that coordinate with the patterned paper.

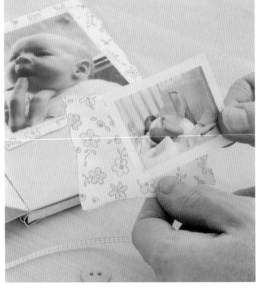

9 Create frames on other pages for your photos to soften the edges and blend them into the background. Cut parchment paper slightly larger than the photo and then tear a piece of baby patterned paper larger still. Dab pink ink around the edges of the torn paper. Arrange the mounted photos on the pages and then embellish with sheer ribbon, rickrack braid, baby charms and a little tag.

10 To make a little door for the hidden compartment, cut a 10cm (4in) square of baby patterned paper, then cut a 5.5cm (2¼in) aperture in the centre. Cut around the frame with scallop-edged scissors. Cut a 7cm (2¾in) square of acetate and stick behind the aperture. Attach two pieces of gingham ribbon to the top of the frame, with a nappy (diaper) pin embellishment, and position the door over the compartment, then stick the ribbon onto the album page so that it acts as a hinge. Here, a similar frame has been created for the photo on the opposite page, with a small parchment paper envelope decorated with pink ribbon and rickrack braid added to finish.

11 Tear a piece of baby patterned paper to fit the front of the album, then tear a band of plainer pink paper to fit across the centre. Machine stitch two rows of zigzag stitches to secure the papers. Embellish the paper panel with ribbon. Transfer the pram template on page 99 onto white paper and colour in with colouring pens or pencils. Stick onto white lightweight card and cut out, leaving a narrow border. Apply Dimensional Magic™ to highlight some of the coloured areas and leave to dry. Stick the pram in the centre of the paper panel. Add gingham ribbon to the sides of the panel and then stick on the front of the album. Tie the ribbon at the side and trim to length.

Tiny Tot's Trinket Tin

YOU WILL NEED

- round tin box with lid
- pink baby patterned papers – shoe, floral
- white tissue paper
- white acrylic gesso
- pink and white acrylic paint
- inkpads – 2–3 shades of pink
- 15cm (6in) of 6mm (¼in) wide deep pink satin ribbon
- 50cm (20in) of 6mm (¼in) wide pale pastel organza ribbon – 3 shades
- baby shoe and nappy (diaper) pin card embellishments
- sponge dauber or cosmetic sponge
- pink sewing thread and needle or sewing machine
- Basic Tool Kit (see page 6)

1 Paint the outside of the tin box and lid with white acrylic gesso and leave to dry. Mix the pink and white paint to a pale shade of pink and paint the box and lid. Leave to dry. Using two or three shades of pink ink and a sponge dauber or cosmetic sponge, dab colour over the outside of the box and lid, applying darker pink around the edges. Leave to dry.

2 Tear pairs of baby shoes from the shoe patterned paper and slightly larger squares of the floral patterned paper. Dab around the edges of the patches with the pink inks. Use just a dot of glue to stick the shoes on the floral patches and then sew a square border around the shoes with pink thread, either by hand or machine.

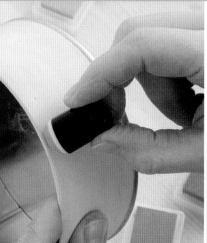

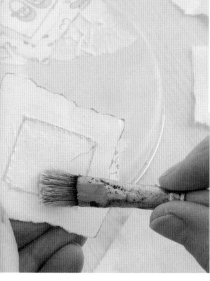

3 Apply Mod Podge™ or PVA (white) glue diluted with water to the reverse of the patches. Stick on the lid. Crush torn pieces of tissue paper and stick between the patches. Tear a narrow band of floral patterned paper and colour the edges with pink ink. Stick around the base of the box, applying tissue paper as before.

4 Punch a 1.5mm (¹⁄₁₆in) hole in the lid centre with a holepunch and hammer (cut a same-size paper circle and fold in quarters to find the centre). Punch holes at the quarter lines near the outer edge and four in between. Thread a satin ribbon loop through the centre hole and tie in a knot. Stick pairs of shoes together at the ends of the organza ribbon. Stick the nappy (diaper) pin heads back to back and tie onto the organza ribbon. Thread through the remaining holes and tie at different lengths.

Mother's Day Magic

Although the timing may differ depending on the country, Mother's Day is celebrated all over the world. Making small posies of pretty flowers and handmade cards is the traditional way to give thanks on this special day, or try this dynamic and contemporary approach.

Make a real impact with a decorative ribbon-tied card that opens to reveal a surprise bouquet of flowers. For a mum who is young at heart, make or decorate a gift box with a trendy pop-up handbag on the lid, jazzed-up with sheer ribbon, fancy yarn and novelty buttons for an extra-special effect. While any self-respecting follower of fashion today can't have too many handbags, a fan was the 'must-have' accessory in the Victorian era, and fan-shaped greetings cards were all the rage. This elegant card unties and opens out to reveal its secret cache of favourite photos – the ideal way to say just how much all those precious years of being in your mum's company mean to you.

Pop-out Posy The impact of the pop-up is enhanced by using boldly patterned card for the flowers, which contrasts with the paler colour of the background.

Bags of Love The fun handbag decoration on the box lid hides a small pop-up handbag beneath, which is sure to delight mum as she unties the ribbon bow and lifts up the bag.

Mum's Biggest Fan Imagine the happy memories that your mum will experience when she unties the beautiful bow and opens this pretty ribbon-strung fan to discover its surprise montage of family photos.

Pop-out Posy

YOU WILL NEED

- plain pink medium card 20 x 14.5cm (8 x 5¾in)
- scrap of white striped watermark paper
- pink patterned lightweight card 30cm (12in) square – polka dot, spots and circles, spotted
- wine and soft green lightweight card
- scraps of pink and orange lightweight card
- pink ribbed medium card 21 x 16cm (8¼ x 6¼in), scored and folded in half
- inkpads – pink, wine and olive green
- pink craft wire
- 64cm (25in) of 7mm (⅜in) wide grosgrain ribbon
- 1cm (½in) circle punch (optional)
- wire cutters (optional)
- round-nosed pliers
- Basic Tool Kit (see page 6)

1 Cut a piece of white paper 20 x 14.5cm (8 x 5¾in). Fold in half, open out and then directly trace the pop-up insert on page 99 onto the paper using a sharp pencil, with the centre fold lines matching up. Lay the paper pattern on top of the plain pink card (which is not scored or folded at this stage) and mark the dots on the template on the card with a pin. Using a craft knife against a ruler on a cutting mat, cut along the zigzag horizontal lines marked by the pinholes.

2 Score the vertical lines between the top and bottom pinholes. Score the centre fold line of the card only as far down as the cut zigzag line. Fold the card and carefully push out the pop-out section. Firmly crease along all the lines and check that the card will fold flat.

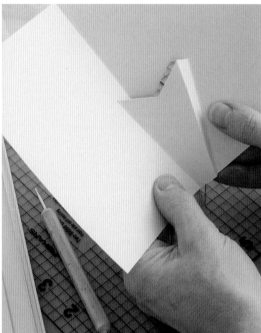

BRIGHT IDEA
If you can't find patterned lightweight card, use patterned papers and stick onto thin card before using them.

3 Using the templates on page 99, cut out a flower from the polka dot and spots and circles patterned card and the wine card, then cut out five leaf shapes from the soft green card. Punch or cut out three 1cm (½in) circles from the wine, pink and orange card and stick in the centre of the flowers. Trace the shape of the pop-out section onto the white striped watermark paper and cut out. Stick in place on the pink card.

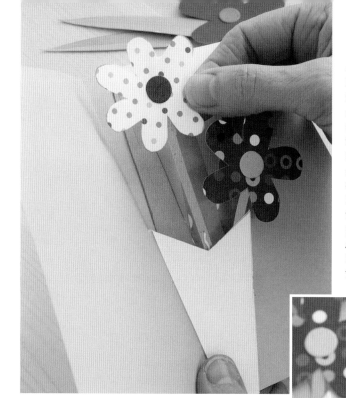

4 Score the leaves down the centre. Using a darker tone of colour than the leaves and flowers, dab ink along and around the edges of each leaf and flower. Stick three of the leaves on the back of the card. Cut three thin strips of soft green card for stems. Stick the flowers onto the stems, then stick the stems behind the pop-out section. Stick the remaining two leaves on the pop-out section behind the flowers. Attach the remaining flower to the back of the card with adhesive foam pads.

BRIGHT IDEA
Thinner craft wire can be cut with scissors if you don't have wire cutters – cut near to the base of the scissors to limit damage to the blades.

5 Cut two 1.5cm (⅝in) wide strips of spotted patterned card. Stick one close to the right-hand edge of the card and one down the centre of the left-hand side. Cut a 2.5 x 4cm (1 x 1½in) rectangle of soft green card. Stick a 1.5cm (⅝in) wide strip of spotted patterned card down the centre and then trim the top corners to make a small tag. Punch a small hole at the top. Thread a length of pink craft wire through the hole. Twist the wires together and then coil each end with pliers. Stick a length of the ribbon across the pop-out section and trim neatly. Attach the tag.

6 Stick double-sided tape around the edge of the pop-up card on the reverse side. Stick one or two pieces near the centre fold. Peel off part of the backing paper from the outer tape and all of it from the pieces on the fold. Position the card inside the pink ribbed card, peel off the remaining backing paper and press in place to stick.

7 Stick a 50cm (20in) length of ribbon across the back of the card just above the centre. Tie in a bow on the front of the card to one side. Cut a 6 x 9.5cm (2⅜ x 3¾in) piece of soft green card. Attach a 5 x 9.5cm (2 x 3¾in) piece of spotted patterned card centrally on top. Trim the top corners to make a tag and punch a small hole at the top. Thread through the remaining ribbon, tie in a knot and trim the ends at an angle. Tuck the tag under the ribbon to finish.

If you like, you could use rubdown letters to add 'Mum', 'Mother' or 'Mummy' to the tag on the front of the card.

21

Mum's Biggest Fan

YOU WILL NEED

- grey board 20 x 15cm (8 x 6in)
- grey/orange/pink patterned lightweight card 30cm (12in) square – leaf print, polka dot, striped
- grey, orange, pink, wine and beige lightweight card
- family photos
- 20cm (8in) of deep pink and orange rickrack braid
- 50cm (20in) of 7mm (⅜in) wide sheer wine ribbon
- 50cm (20in) of 1.5cm (⅝in) wide sheer wine ribbon
- contrasting sewing thread and needle or sewing machine
- Basic Tool Kit (see page 6)

1 To draw the fan shapes onto the grey board, mark 4cm (1½in) in from the left-hand edge and the top and bottom edges. Mark 8cm (3⅛in) in from the top left-hand corner. Mark 1.8cm (¾in) either side of the 4cm (1½in) mark along the bottom edge. Join the left-hand one of these marks to the top left-hand corner and the right-hand one to the 8cm (3⅛in) mark on the top edge to create a fan shape. Rotate the board and repeat to draw a second fan shape.

2 Cut out both fan shapes with a craft knife against a metal safety ruler on a cutting mat. Use one of the fan shapes to draw around and cut out the front fan panel from the leaf print patterned card. Cut out five more fan panels from the toning colours of card.

3 Choose suitable photos. You can scan colour photos into a home computer and use a software program to remove the colour to create black and white pictures. If necessary, crop into the part of the images you want, then alter the size to suit the project. Print out the pictures onto glossy photographic paper using a colour printer for best results. Arrange one of the photos on a centre fan panel, leaving 3mm (⅛in) of paper showing on the right-hand side. Trim the left-hand side of the photo at an angle to align with the edge of the fan panel.

BRIGHT IDEA
It doesn't matter that you have now grown up – select favourite photos of you and your brothers and sisters over the years.

4 Repeat the process with the remaining photos, altering the position of each photo to create a visual balance across the fan. Decorate the fan panels with strips of coordinating patterned card – here, pink shades were used for the girl pictures and orange shades for the boy pictures. Cut pieces of deep pink and orange rickrack braid and stick onto the panels. Sew in place with a contrasting shade of thread, either by hand or machine, then trim neatly.

5 Cover the two grey board fan panels with white paper. To do this, stick the paper on one side and trim to 1cm (½in) all round. Cut diagonally across the corners, 2mm (¹⁄₁₆in) from the edge of the card. Stick the long sides down on the reverse side and then tuck in the tiny edges of paper at the corners before sticking the paper down at the short ends. Stick the front and back panels of the fan onto these prepared board panels.

6 Decorate the front panel with a wide strip of polka dot patterned card and narrower strips of orange card. Punch holes through the bottom of the front fan panel. Use this panel to mark the position of the hole on the back panel and on the centre panels and punch out. Place the fan panels in order and thread through a folded 15cm (6in) length of the narrow ribbon. Tuck the ribbon ends through the loop to secure.

7 Missing out the front panel, stick 5.5cm (2¼in) lengths of the narrow ribbon to the top left-hand corner of the next fan panel. Turn the fan over and open it out so that the panels overlap exactly where you want. Stick the ribbon on the back right-hand corner of the front panel. Repeat for each fan panel. Stick the wider ribbon on the back of the fan and use to tie the fan closed with a bow at the front.

Keep the embellishment on the front of the fan subtle to increase the surprise element once it is opened out.

23

Bags of Love

YOU WILL NEED

- grey board A4 (US letter)
- patterned paper 30cm (12in) square – polka dot, Lexington print, dots and circles
- wine and orange lightweight card
- 60cm (24in) of 7mm (³⁄₈in) wide sheer orange ribbon
- 20cm (8in) of orange fancy yarn
- 2 orange flower buttons
- Basic Tool Kit (see page 6)

1 For the box base, draw an 11.5 x 19cm (4½ x 7½in) rectangle onto the grey board. Draw a line 1.8cm (¾in) in from each edge. Using a craft knife against a metal safety ruler on a cutting mat, cut out around the outer lines and cut away each corner square. Score along the inner lines and fold up the sides. Stick the corners together with narrow strips of white paper and PVA (white) glue.

2 For the lid, draw a 12.5 x 20cm (5 x 8in) rectangle onto the grey board. Draw a line 2.5cm (1in) in from each edge, cut out and make up as for the box base. Cover the inside of the two box sections with white paper so that the paper ends 3mm (¹⁄₈in) from the top edge. Add 6mm (¼in) all round to the outer box base and lid dimensions (before they were made up) to calculate the sizes to cover the lid and base. Use the polka dot patterned paper to cover the outside of the lid and white paper for the base, cutting only part of the corner section away to leave a tab for sticking. Stick each tab on the inside, directly onto the box.

BRIGHT IDEA

Look out for coordinating ranges of paper that have a plain colour on one side and a toning pattern on the other side.

3 Enlarge the large handbag template on page 100 on a photocopier or computer according to the percentage specified. Trace or print out onto the Lexington print patterned paper. Turn over the tracing paper or template and draw a mirror image adjoining the first handbag. Cut out the double handbag shape as one piece. Repeat with the dots and circles patterned paper. Score and fold along the centre line of each double handbag shape, then unfold. Using the template on page 100, cut out the flap and strap from wine card.

4 Reserve a short length of the orange ribbon, then cut the remaining ribbon in half. Stick the two double handbag shapes together back to back, tucking one piece of ribbon between the layers in the centre at each end. Stick double-sided tape onto the Lexington-print side on one end of the handbag shape only. Attach to the box lid so that there is an equal space between the opened handbag and the short edges of the box at both ends.

5 Using the template on page 100, cut the small handbag shape from polka dot patterned paper and score along the dotted lines. Cut the slits along the centre fold for the yarn handle as marked on the template. Tuck one end of a short length of yarn through one slit and stick on the inside, then tuck the other end of the yarn into the remaining slit and stick in place. Cut a heart from orange card and stick on the front of the small handbag. Using double-sided tape, stick the tabs of the small handbag onto the opened large handbag so that the tabs butt up to one another along the centre fold line.

6 Stick the bag strap onto the box lid and the bag flap to the front of the bag. Cut a short length of yarn for the front of the bag. Fold the yarn and the reserved ribbon in half and stick on the flap. Attach a button on top and a second button to the bag strap.

When the bow is untied to reveal the pop-up bag inside, retie the ribbon underneath the box to hold it in place.

An Easter Extravaganza

People all round the world celebrate new life and new beginnings at Easter by decorating eggs, its most identifiable symbol, in different ways. Easter is one of the oldest festivals, so join in the springtime festivities with fresh inspiration from these fun twists on tradition.

If you haven't time to go hunting Easter eggs, create this delightful card with a hidden egg surprise – it's really easy to make and guaranteed to raise a smile. Turn a little gift of tiny chocolate eggs into an extra-special treat with a cleverly constructed egg box using bright spring colours such as yellow, green and orange for the box and pretty coordinating prints for the egg shapes. Being a spring festival, it's traditional to decorate bonnets with fresh flowers at Easter. Try using these delightfully simple tissue flowers instead or give someone a real 'spring' surprise as they suddenly pop up from a pot.

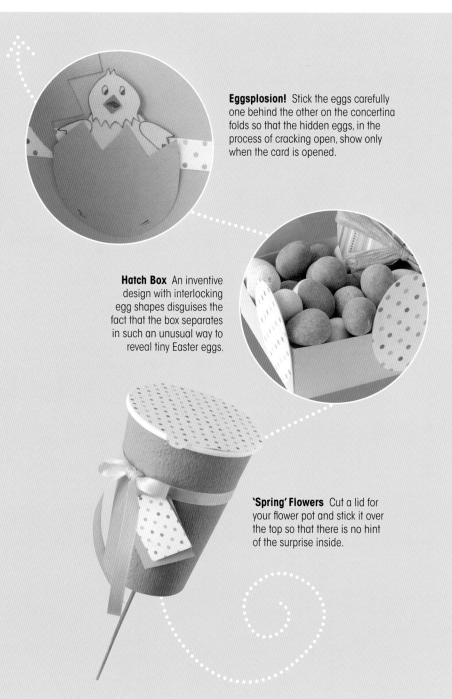

Eggsplosion! Stick the eggs carefully one behind the other on the concertina folds so that the hidden eggs, in the process of cracking open, show only when the card is opened.

Hatch Box An inventive design with interlocking egg shapes disguises the fact that the box separates in such an unusual way to reveal tiny Easter eggs.

'Spring' Flowers Cut a lid for your flower pot and stick it over the top so that there is no hint of the surprise inside.

Eggsplosion!

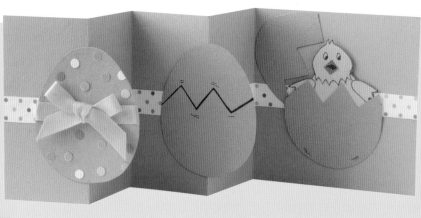

YOU WILL NEED

- bright green card
- polka dot patterned paper
- bright pink cross-hatch textured card
- scraps of bright pastel card
- yellow card
- bright orange paper
- dark green fine-line pen
- 30cm (12in) of 7mm (⅜in) wide yellow satin ribbon
- 6mm (¼in) circle punch
- Basic Tool Kit (see page 6)

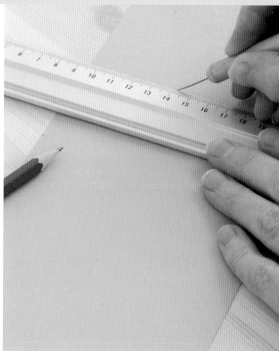

1 Cut a 30 x 10cm (12 x 4in) strip of bright green card. Mark at four 5cm (2in) intervals from the left-hand side along the top and bottom edges. Score down the strip to join each set of marks.

2 Cut a 30 x 1.5cm (12 x ⅝in) strip of polka dot patterned paper and stick across the centre of the card. Make a valley fold along the right-hand score line, then make a mountain fold along the next score line. Continue folding along the remaining score lines to form a concertina.

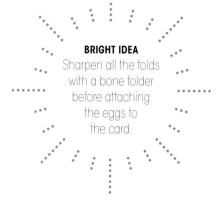

BRIGHT IDEA
Sharpen all the folds with a bone folder before attaching the eggs to the card.

3 Transfer the egg template on page 100 onto white lightweight card and use to cut three eggs from the pink textured card. Cut along the zigzag line on the template and use the shape to draw a zigzag pencil line across two of the pink eggs.

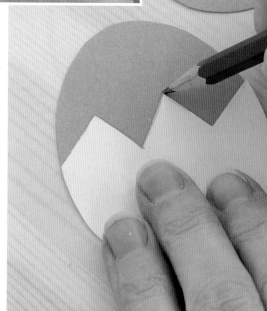

4 Using the circle punch, punch different-coloured spots from the card scraps and stick all over the remaining pink egg. Stick the length of ribbon across the back of the egg and then tie in a bow at the front. Trim the ends of the ribbon bow neatly. Stick the decorated egg centrally on the front fold of the card.

5 Using the template on page 100, draw the chick sections onto yellow card. Add the details as marked on the template with the green pen, including the diamond shape in the centre of the beak. Cut out the sections. Cut the beak from bright orange paper and stick in place.

6 Assemble the chick with PVA (white) glue. Cut along the zigzag line on one egg. Check the height of the chick so that it fits within the whole egg shape and then stick in position behind the lower half of the egg. Stick the egg and chick on the back panel of the green card so that it is hidden behind the front egg. Stick the top half of the egg on the left-hand side of the panel.

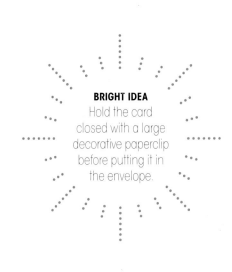

7 Draw along the zigzag line on the remaining egg with the green pen, widening the line so that it looks like the crack is beginning to open. Mark 'wobble' lines as shown in the photo. Stick the egg on the centre panel of the card so that it is hidden behind the front egg.

BRIGHT IDEA
Hold the card closed with a large decorative paperclip before putting it in the envelope.

Hatch Box

YOU WILL NEED

- textured card – bright yellow, bright orange
- patterned paper – polka dot, striped
- bright green raffia or ribbon
- Basic Tool Kit (see page 6)

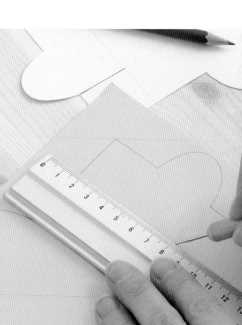

1 Transfer the box shape on page 101 onto white lightweight card and cut out to make a template. If you are tracing, draw on the slightly heavier lines, which indicate slits, and dashed lines to show the fold lines. Draw around the template onto the yellow and orange card. Mark the position of the dashed lines without actually drawing them on.

2 Score across the box outline between the marks as indicated by the dashed lines on the template. Cut the two box shapes out carefully along the outside edge.

3 Transfer the egg template on page 100 onto white lightweight card and use to cut four eggs from polka dot patterned paper and another four eggs from striped patterned paper.

BRIGHT IDEA
Keep the box shapes the same way up and stick the eggs on the right side so that the two halves of the box link together.

4 Apply PVA (white) glue to the reverse side of the eggs. Check that the eggs are the right way up before sticking the polka dot eggs onto the yellow box shape and then the striped eggs onto the orange box shape.

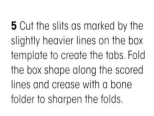

5 Cut the slits as marked by the slightly heavier lines on the box template to create the tabs. Fold the box shape along the scored lines and crease with a bone folder to sharpen the folds.

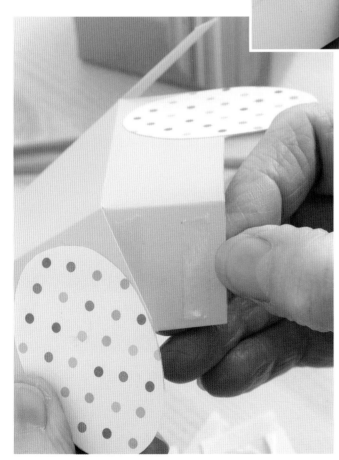

6 Apply double-sided tape to the tabs. Peel off the backing paper and stick in place inside the box. Repeat to make the orange box. Fill one box with Easter goodies and shredded tissue paper, then link the two halves of the box together so that all the egg shapes are visible on the outside. Wrap a length of green raffia or ribbon around the box to secure and tie in a bow at the front.

Raffia or ribbon tied around the box keeps it closed and adds a decorative touch.

'Spring' Flowers

YOU WILL NEED

- tissue papers – white, pale yellow, yellow, orange
- green crepe paper
- polka dot patterned paper
- green marker pen (optional)
- white and orange acrylic paint
- 4 green pipe cleaners
- bamboo skewer or green fine garden cane
- 2 paper cups, about 11.5cm (4½in) high, 9cm (3⅓in) diameter
- Basic Tool Kit (see page 6)

1 Cut six 10cm (4in) squares from each of the different colours of tissue paper. Layer the tissue paper into three piles, beginning with two sheets of white, then two pale yellow, two yellow and two orange. Fold each pile in half and shape the ends with scissors. The shaping is optional, but gives a better finish to the flowers.

2 Take one pile and, keeping the papers folded in half, fold in each side twice to create a concertina. Cut a 'v' shape in the centre of the cut-edge side and secure the folds with a pipe cleaner, leaving one long end. Repeat with the two remaining piles of tissue paper.

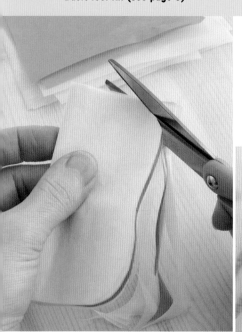

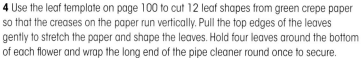

3 Open out the concertina slightly and then gently pull up the first layer of orange tissue paper. Pull both orange petals up so that they are fairly upright, and then pull up the other layers of tissue, one at time, to create the flowers.

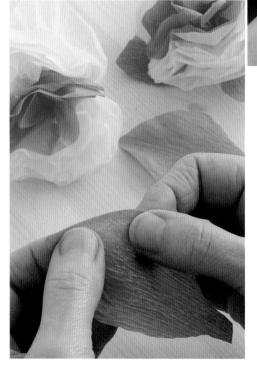

4 Use the leaf template on page 100 to cut 12 leaf shapes from green crepe paper so that the creases on the paper run vertically. Pull the top edges of the leaves gently to stretch the paper and shape the leaves. Hold four leaves around the bottom of each flower and wrap the long end of the pipe cleaner round once to secure.

5 Colour the bamboo skewer with a green marker pen and leave to dry, or use a green fine garden cane. Trim two of the long ends of pipe cleaner and then stick the flowers, one at a time, around the top of the skewer or cane. Wrap the remaining long end of pipe cleaner around the base of the flowers to secure.

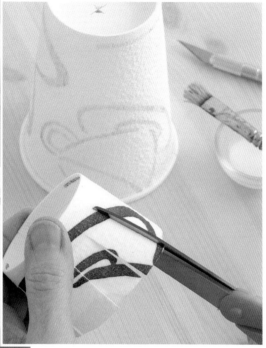

6 Mark the centre of the base of each paper cup and cut a small cross at each mark with the point of a craft knife. To create a support for the flower stem, cut one of the paper cups down to 3cm (1¼in) high and cut slits around the edge. Stick upside down inside the other paper cup using strong glue.

7 Paint the cups with one or two coats of white acrylic paint to cover any pattern and leave to dry. Paint with orange acrylic paint and again leave to dry.

8 To make the lid of the pot, turn the paper cup upside down and draw around it onto polka dot patterned paper. Cut out with a small tab at one side. Feed the flower stem down through the hole inside the cup and out of the hole in the base. Gently press the flowers together so that they fit inside the cup and push down until they are hidden. Stick the lid over the top of the cup with a very fine line of PVA (white) glue.

BRIGHT IDEA
Use the type of paper cup that you get with take-away coffee or milk shakes.

'Spring' Flowers · 33

Father's Day Thrills

Father's Day, first celebrated in the USA in 1910 and now popular the world over, is the time for children, no matter what age, to show Dad just how special he is. What better way than with an imaginative handmade gift with an unexpected element.

Entertain your dad with a card that is sure to catch him by surprise when it lands a prize fish in dramatic pop-up style. Although one of the simplest pop-up mechanisms, it's really effective. Add novelty value to a gift bag containing his favourite tipple with an elegant tie tag that pulls open to reveal the treat in store. If you are feeling more adventurous in your creative endeavours, make Dad's day truly memorable with a unique photo frame ingeniously designed around the wheel and dashboard of a classic sports car. What better way than to give a fantastic handmade gift with a fun surprise that reflects his favourite hobby or pastime.

Card with a Catch The smart, business-like exterior of this card only serves to heighten the surprise factor as a fish comes flying out when the card is opened.

Best-dressed Bottle The ends of this tag pull apart to reveal a fun motif hidden inside. Try other designs such as a beer mug to suit your dad's preferences.

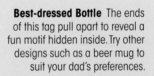

The Drive of His Life Even if this is the nearest your dad will get to a sports car, he'll have fun turning the steering wheel to reveal the hidden family photos.

Card with a Catch

YOU WILL NEED

- cream card
- fish patterned paper
- blue vellum – 2 shades
- blue card
- square spotted patterned paper
- rust-coloured paper
- blue and rust fine marker pens
- fine cord or string
- tweezers
- liquid vellum adhesive
- circle punches – 6mm (¼in) and 2.5cm (1in)
- 3 rust-coloured eyelets
- sewing thread and needle
- corner punch (optional)
- Basic Tool Kit (see page 6)

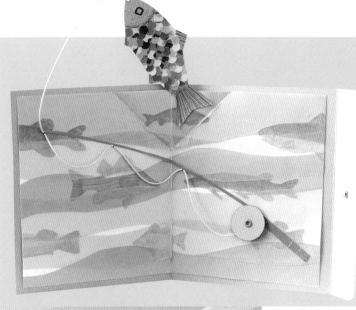

1 Cut a 21.5 x 12cm (8½ x 4¾in) piece of cream card. Cut out a few fish from the fish patterned paper with small, pointed scissors and use tweezers to stick all over the cream card. Trim any fish overlapping the card to align with the edge.

2 Cut wavy strips from the two different shades of blue vellum to fit across the card. Stick to the card using vellum adhesive and leave to dry.

BRIGHT IDEA

Look for liquid vellum adhesive, which is generally stronger than dry adhesive, for this card, so that the vellum adheres firmly.

3 Using the template on page 101, cut a fish from blue card. Punch lots of 6mm (¼in) circles in a range of colours from the square spotted patterned paper. Stick the circles onto the fish in rows, beginning at the tail end. Overlap the second and subsequent rows so that the circles resemble scales. Leave to dry and then trim neatly.

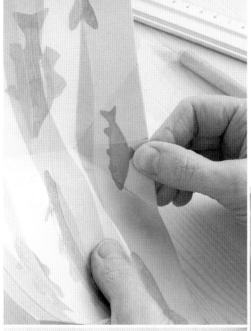

4 Score the vellum-covered card down the centre. Mark 4cm (1½in) down the score line from the top edge and also 4cm (1½in) out to both sides. Score to join the marks and create a 'v' shape. Pull the 'v' shape out to form the pop-up mechanism, then close the card and go along the fold lines with a bone folder to sharpen the creases.

BRIGHT IDEA
To make sewing easier, punch holes with a paper pricker where you want to stitch the cord onto the fishing rod.

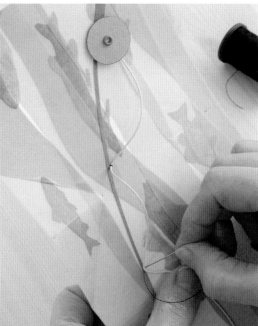

5 Cut a thin tapered strip of rust-coloured paper to make a fishing rod and stick diagonally across the card. Cut a wider strip for the handle. Punch a 2.5cm (1in) circle from blue card and set a rust-coloured eyelet in the centre (see Step 2, page 52). Attach a length of fine cord or string to the back and then stick onto the fishing rod using adhesive foam pads. Sew the fine cord or string onto the rod in three places, including the tip.

6 Colour the fish tail and fins with fine marker pens. Add an eye punched from the square spotted patterned paper. Stick the fish tail on the right-hand side of the 'v' fold. Attach the end of the fishing line behind the fish's mouth.

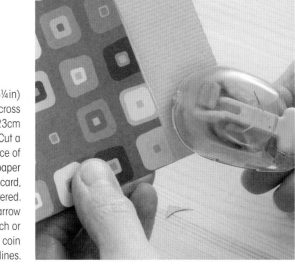

7 Cut a 26.5 x 13cm (10½ x 5¼in) piece of blue card. Score across the card 11.5cm (4½in) and 23cm (9in) from one short side. Cut a 23 x 13cm (9 x 5¼in) piece of square spotted patterned paper and stick to the back of the card, leaving the narrow flap uncovered. Round the corners of the narrow flap section with a corner punch or draw the curves using a small coin and cut along the lines.

8 Punch two 2.5cm (1in) circles from blue card and stick a length of fine cord or string behind one. Fold up the card and mark the position of the circles on the flap and main section with a pin. Open the card out and attach the circles with rust eyelets. Stick the pop-up card inside the folder using double-sided tape.

Best-dressed Bottle

YOU WILL NEED

- **grey board**
- **blue patterned papers – spotted, striped**
- **scrap of gold card**
- **large sheet of blue stardream paper or strong wrapping paper**
- **blue card**
- **blue inkpad**
- **black fine-line pen**
- **colouring pens**
- **raffia or paper string**
- **sponge dauber or cosmetic sponge**
- **Basic Tool Kit (see page 6)**

1 To make the tag, cut six 5cm (2in) squares from grey board. On two of the squares, draw lines 7mm (⅜in) in from the sides and up from the bottom edge. Mark a further 4mm (⅛in) in from each 7mm (⅜in) side line on the bottom edge. Cut out the four 'L' shapes and stick on the sides of two of the other squares. Add a thin strip of card to fill the gap between the 'L' shapes at the top on each prepared square.

2 Cut a scant 3.5 x 9cm (1¼ x 3½in) piece of grey board. Draw a line 4mm (⅛in) from each long side edge and 7mm (⅜in) from the top and bottom edges. Cut out the narrow side strips to create the slider bar. Stick a panel of spotted patterned paper on the front of the slider. Place the slider bar into a prepared square at each end, then stick the remaining two grey board squares on top, around three sides only, allowing the slider to move freely.

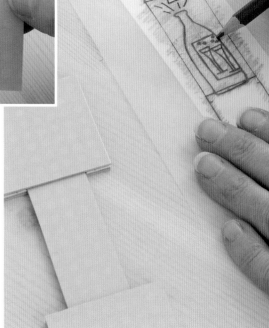

BRIGHT IDEA
Measure and cut the grey board sections as accurately as possible so that the slide mechanism isn't too tight or too loose.

3 Attach two lengths of raffia or paper string to the top square. Stick a square of spotted patterned paper on the front of the top and bottom squares. Using a sponge dauber or cosmetic sponge, dab all the edges of the tag with blue ink. Transfer the bottle template on page 101 onto white paper. Outline with a black fine-line pen and then colour in. Cut out and trim the bottom 3mm (⅛in) from the bottle, as marked with a dashed line on the template (put this piece safely on one side for later). Stick the bottle on the fully opened slider bar.

4 Using the template on page 101, cut out the tie sections from striped patterned paper. Stick them onto the squares aligned with the slider bar. Stick just the tab of the tie knot in place. Use an adhesive foam pad to raise the tie knot. Stick the reserved bottom part of the bottle in place. Using the templates on page 101, cut the cork from gold card and stick the top half only onto the top part of the tag. Cut two collars from white paper. Apply glue to the folded-over edges and secure in position, with foam adhesive pads under the points.

BRIGHT IDEA
To make paper string handles, twist several lengths of paper raffia together.

5 To make the bottle bag, cut a 33 x 43cm (13 x 17in) piece of stardream paper or strong wrapping paper. Mark along both short sides at 1cm, 8cm, 8cm and 8cm intervals (½in, 3⅛in, 3⅛in and 3⅛in). Fold between the marks and firmly crease. Stick the 1cm (½in) flap under the other long edge and lay flat.

6 Fold down 3cm (1⅛in) and then a further 3.5cm (1½in) at the top. Fold up 4cm (1½in) at the bottom end, then open out the bag and fold in the bottom edges neatly as shown. Cut a square slightly less than 8cm (3⅛in) from the stardream paper or wrapping paper and also one from blue card. Tuck the blue card square inside the bag and stick the stardream paper or wrapping paper square on the bottom of the bag.

7 Open out the bag and turn the top edge to the inside twice along the pre-creased folds. Fold two opposite sides of the bag inwards as shown. Cut two 8 x 3cm (3⅛ x 1⅛in) pieces of the stardream paper or wrapping paper. Stick a length of raffia or paper string in a loop onto each strip. Stick the strips inside the top of the bag, sandwiching the raffia or string between the strips and the bag.

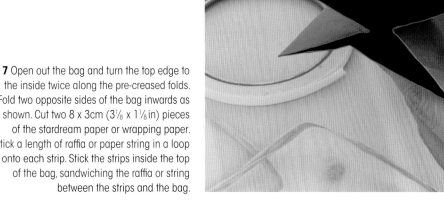

Best-dressed Bottle • 39

The Drive of His Life

1 Trace the outline of the half steering wheel template on page 102 (excluding the dashboard marked in pale grey) onto tracing paper. Scribble along the lines on the reverse side with a soft (B) pencil. Lay the template on the grey board and draw over the half steering wheel, marking the outer solid line and bottom triangular shape on the right-hand side, but omitting the indicator lever. Flip the template and draw the second side, with the indicator lever on the left-hand side. Mark and draw only two diagonally opposite triangular shapes.

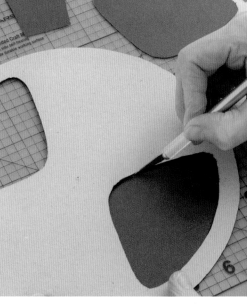

2 Cut out the steering wheel and the two triangular shapes along the solid line using a craft knife. Spread glue over one side of the steering wheel and stick onto the stardream paper. With the card side up, cut out around the outside edge of the steering wheel and inside the two triangular shapes.

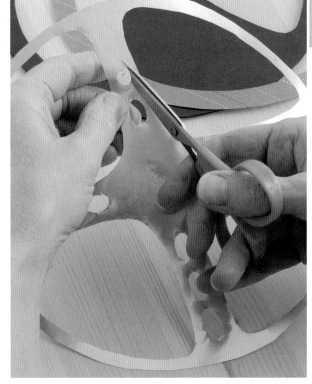

3 Trace the rim of the steering wheel onto blue striped patterned paper and cut out. Trace the whole steering wheel out as far as the dashed line onto the front of silver self-adhesive foil and cut out. Cut out the small ovals using small, pointed scissors. Check the position of the foil so that it matches the two cutouts. Peel off the backing paper and stick the foil in place on the board steering wheel. Stick the blue striped wheel rim on top.

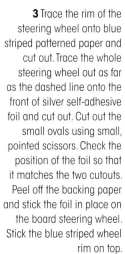

BRIGHT IDEA
Lay textured card face down on the silver foil and hammer with a rubber hammer to create a speckled effect.

4 Trace the dashboard template on page 102, indicated by the pale grey line, onto grey board as described in Step 1, flipping the template to draw the second side. Draw the indicator lever on the right-hand side. Cut out around the edge. Stick the card onto the stardream paper and cut away the excess paper.

BRIGHT IDEA
Cut around the edges of the photos neatly, as the edges will be seen when the wheel is turned to reveal the alternative images.

5 Choose photos to go behind the steering wheel cutouts. You will need four altogether. Enlarge or reduce the images so that they fit inside the cutouts. Cut out a triangular shape from the tracing paper template and use this as a guide to trim the photos. Stick the photos on the dashboard panel so that two fit inside the triangular windows and the other two are revealed when the steering wheel is turned.

6 Cut a circle from blue striped patterned paper to fit in the centre of the steering wheel, as indicated on the template. Stick in place. Punch a hole in the centre. Using a set of compasses or punches, cut or punch two 1.5cm (⅝in) and two 4.5cm (1¾in) circles from white paper. Mark up the circles with the blue pen to resemble dials on the dashboard. Stick the circles onto the blue striped paper and cut out to leave a border. Stick the dials in place. Attach the steering wheel with the paper fastener (brad) through the centre.

7 Cut a 6 x 21cm (2⅜ x 8¼in) strip of grey board for a stand. Score across it at 2cm, 2.5cm, 2.5cm and 12cm (¾in, 1in, 1in and 4¾in) intervals. Fold the stand along the scored lines as shown in the photo. Stick the lower tab onto the bottom edge of the dashboard on the reverse, then flatten the stand and stick the top flap in place on the reverse of the wheel.

Choose photos of your favourite happy memories to fit the shape of the cutouts.

Wedding Wonders

Marriages are celebrated differently the world over, but while every ceremony has its own traditions and customs, each focuses on the happiness and wellbeing of the lucky couple. These inspirational and versatile design ideas can be adapted to suit any style of wedding.

What wedding would be complete without a cake? The classic tiered cake is the perfect greetings card motif for sending best wishes to the bride and groom. Dress up the wedding table with these quick and easy little favours boxes. Traditionally filled with five almonds to signify health, wealth, fertility, happiness and long life, favours boxes are a thoughtful way of thanking guests for their support and gifts. Then why not use some of the photos from the day to make a lasting memento? Lace from the wedding dress, ribbon from the bridesmaids' dresses and buttons from the pageboys' outfits can be used to embellish the pictures. Together with a stunning photo of the bride and groom concealed behind the doors, this is the opening page of a truly memorable scrapbook.

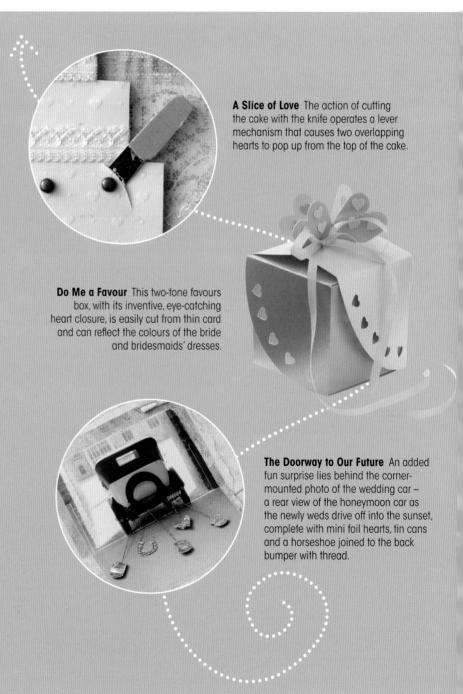

A Slice of Love The action of cutting the cake with the knife operates a lever mechanism that causes two overlapping hearts to pop up from the top of the cake.

Do Me a Favour This two-tone favours box, with its inventive, eye-catching heart closure, is easily cut from thin card and can reflect the colours of the bride and bridesmaids' dresses.

The Doorway to Our Future An added fun surprise lies behind the corner-mounted photo of the wedding car – a rear view of the honeymoon car as the newly weds drive off into the sunset, complete with mini foil hearts, tin cans and a horseshoe joined to the back bumper with thread.

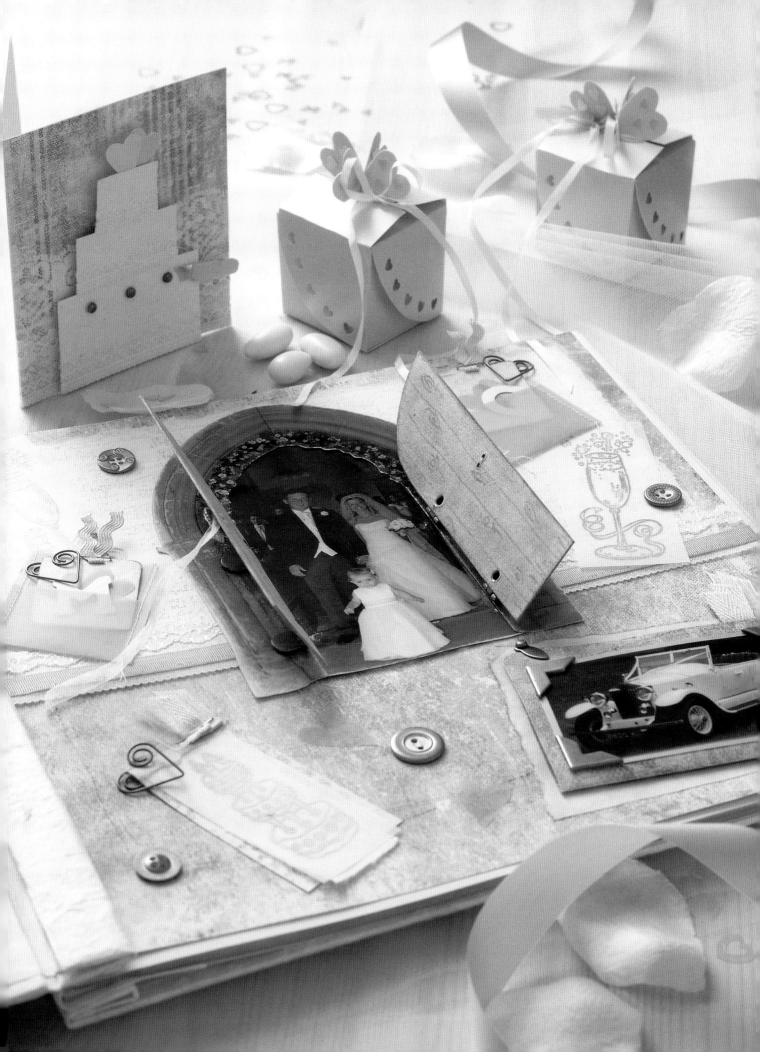

A Slice of Love

YOU WILL NEED

- cream medium card 22 x 12cm (8½ x 4¾in)
- music collage paper
- hearts and dots vellum
- silver mirror heavyweight card
- scraps of blue and cream pearlized card
- 40cm (16in) of 3cm (1¼in) wide cream lace
- vellum adhesive
- 4 pewter small paper fasteners (brads)
- Basic Tool Kit (see page 6)

1 Score the cream card widthways across the centre and fold. Cut the music collage paper to fit the front of the folded card. Stick a piece of lace across the bottom of the paper and stick the ends on the reverse side. Stick the paper onto the card.

2 Trace or photocopy the cake template on page 105 onto white lightweight card and cut out. Cut a 10cm (4in) square of the hearts and dots vellum and stick onto a same-size square of white medium card using vellum adhesive. Draw around the cake template on the reverse side and cut out.

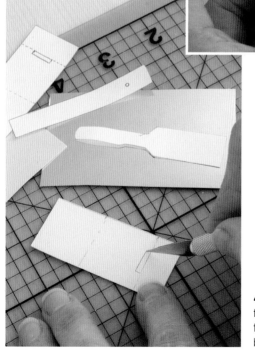

3 Lay the template on the right side of the vellum-covered card and mark the holes and the curved slot as marked on the template with a pin. Punch 2mm (1/16in) holes and carefully cut along the slot line with a craft knife. Trim the remaining lace to create graduated widths and use to decorate the cake tiers, sticking the ends on the reverse side.

4 Using the templates on page 105, cut out one slot card and two slider-bar strips from white medium card. Transfer the markings as indicated on the templates. Cut the knife shape from silver mirror card. Stick the two slider-bar strips together back to back to strengthen. Punch 2mm (1/16in) holes where indicated and cut the wide slot.

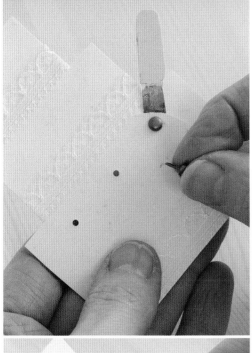

5 Cut a piece of blue pearlized card for the knife handle and stick onto the knife shape. Insert the knife handle through the curved slot in the cake from the reverse side and secure with a pewter paper fastener (brad). Insert paper fasteners (brads) in the other two holes on the front of the cake.

BRIGHT IDEA
If you aren't too confident, you could try out the pop-up mechanism by making a rough mock-up before the final card.

6 Stick double-sided tape on the slot card below the slot only. Peel off the backing paper and stick on the reverse side of the cake so that the dotted lines line up with the cake tiers.

7 Fasten the slider-bar strip to the knife tab with a paper fastener (brad) as shown. Feed the slider bar into the slot. Using the template on page 105, cut out two hearts – one from blue and one from cream pearlized card.

BRIGHT IDEA
To personalize the card, try using pretty rubdown letters to add the couple's initials and wedding date to the cake's tiers.

8 Lower the knife so that the slider bar juts out from the top of the cake. Stick the hearts in place. Check that they disappear when the knife is raised again. Attach the cake to the folded card with adhesive foam pads, making sure that you don't prevent the hearts from moving up and down.

Do Me a Favour

YOU WILL NEED

To make two boxes:
- pearlized card – cream, blue
- scraps of blue pearlized paper
- white or blue narrow silk ribbon
- hand-held small heart punch
- Basic Tool Kit (see page 6)

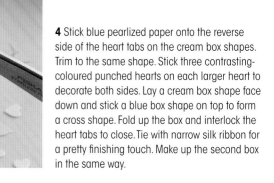

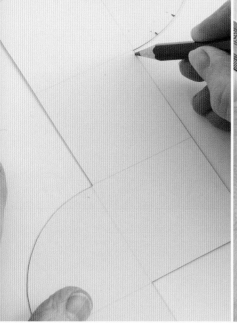

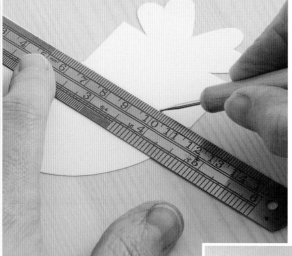

2 Draw around the box outline twice on the reverse side of the blue pearlized card. This time omit the heart shapes at each end, drawing a line straight across, then cut out. Score across the blue and cream box shapes where indicated by the dashed lines on the template.

1 Enlarge the favours box template on page 103 on a photocopier or computer according to the percentage specified. Trace or print out the template onto lightweight card, including the dashed lines and points on the curved edges as marked on the template, and cut out. Lay the template on the reverse side of the cream pearlized card and draw around it twice, one shape below the other. Cut out the boxes along the outline. Cut across halfway under the heart shapes, as indicated by the slightly heavier line on the template.

3 Using the card template as a guide, faintly mark in pencil the points around each of the curved edges on the inside. Punch a small heart at each mark 6mm (¼in) from the edge. Keep the small punched hearts to one side for later.

BRIGHT IDEA
Stick a piece of tape across the punch as a guide to positioning the punch to get a heart exactly 6mm (¼in) from the edge.

4 Stick blue pearlized paper onto the reverse side of the heart tabs on the cream box shapes. Trim to the same shape. Stick three contrasting-coloured punched hearts on each larger heart to decorate both sides. Lay a cream box shape face down and stick a blue box shape on top to form a cross shape. Fold up the box and interlock the heart tabs to close. Tie with narrow silk ribbon for a pretty finishing touch. Make up the second box in the same way.

The Doorway to Our Future...

YOU WILL NEED

- scrapbook album 30cm (12in) square
- blue distressed paper 30cm (12in) square
- cream textured paper
- thin grey board
- blue lace-effect card
- blue pearlized paper
- silver foil
- parchment paper (optional)
- scraps of blue lace-effect paper; cream and off-white card
- blue vellum
- inkpads – VersaMark™, champagne metallic
- stamps – music score, champagne glass, wedding cake, heart leaves
- box of chalks, cotton wool balls and hairspray or artist's fixative
- white acrylic gesso
- fine soft brown felt-tip pen
- wedding photos
- 3cm (1¼in) wide lace
- assorted cream and blue ribbon and rickrack braid
- metal buttons
- 4 metal hinges
- 4 metal photo corners
- photo tab
- heart-shaped paperclips
- punches – corner (optional), letter
- metallic and white sewing thread and sewing machine
- stapler and staples
- Basic Tool Kit (see page 6)

BRIGHT IDEA
If you don't have a photo with a stone arch doorway, simply cut an arch from pretty bridal paper and embellish with stickers.

1 Stick the blue distressed paper to the scrapbook page insert. Cut a 30 x 15cm (12 x 6in) piece of cream textured paper. Using the VersaMark™ inkpad, stamp the music score image all over the cream paper. Beginning with beige at the top and working down to blue, lightly rub chalk all over the paper using cotton wool balls. Set the chalk using hairspray or artist's fixative. Tear the top and side edges, then stick the paper on the top half of the distressed paper.

2 Stick a length of lace across the bottom edge of the stamped paper and stick the ends on the reverse side. Stick the embellished paper on the blue distressed paper. Print out or select the bride and groom photo so that the arch is about 13 x 18cm (5 x 7in). Cut around the arch shape and stick on the scrapbook page.

3 Trace the shape of the doors, following the line inside the arch, and use to cut out two doors from thin grey board. Paint the doors with white acrylic gesso so that the brushstrokes resemble wood grain. Paint the other side once the first side is dry. Colour the doors with chalk to match the photo and then draw in the wood panels and knots with the brown pen.

BRIGHT IDEA
You can use the stamps and embellishments you already have in your work box to decorate the pages.

4 Punch two small holes on each door where handles would be and then tie a button onto each door using sheer ribbon. Tie a length of ribbon behind one button so that you can secure the doors with a figure-of-eight loop. Attach the doors to the scrapbook page using decorative hinges.

BRIGHT IDEA
If you don't have a rear-view photo of the honeymoon car, cut a cartoon car from coloured paper instead.

5 To make the file folder pop-up feature, cut an 11.5 x 16cm (4½ x 6¼in) piece of blue lace-effect card, then score and fold in half. Leaving a 2cm (¾in) tab at the left-hand end, cut 7mm (⅜in) from the front top edge. Round off the corners with scissors or a punch and embellish with ribbons stapled in the top right-hand corner. Print out or select and trim the car photo to fit on the front. Mat the photo onto blue pearlized paper and stick on the front. Embellish with metal photo corners.

6 Trim the rear view photo of the honeymoon car to fit the inside of the file folder and round the corners as in Step 5. Score across just under the wheels so that they will appear to sit on the 'ground'. Stick the photo inside the file folder. Draw some cans, horseshoes and heart shapes in silver foil and cut out. Arrange the foil motifs on the lower half of the photo and stick in place with adhesive foam pads, catching lengths of metallic thread in place at the same time. Sew the threads through the car bumper and secure on the reverse side.

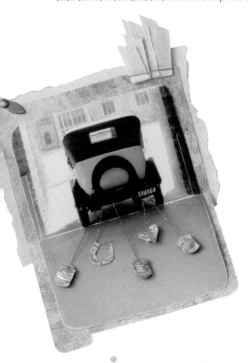

7 Tear a piece of white paper slightly larger than the file folder and colour the edges with blue chalk. Attach the file folder, then stick the panel on the scrapbook page and attach a photo tab to hold the file folder closed.

8 Using the champagne metallic inkpad, stamp two champagne glasses and a wedding cake onto parchment or tracing paper and cut out. Layer the cake image with torn white paper and a piece of blue lace-effect paper. Fold a piece of torn blue vellum over the top edge and machine stitch. Embellish the tag by stapling on several pieces of folded ribbon and attaching a heart-shaped paperclip.

9 Cut two 3.5 x 5cm (1½ x 2in) tag shapes from cream card. Using the VersaMark™ inkpad, stamp the heart leaves image onto each tag. Rub over each image with beige chalks. Dab more ink around the edge and colour with chalks. Set the chalk with hairspray or artist's fixative. Staple a piece of cream rickrack braid on the top.

10 Cut two 5 x 10cm (2 x 4in) pieces of blue vellum and fold up one end to make a pocket. Stitch the side seams with white thread. Decorate the tags with small blue vellum hearts and the initials of the bride and groom punched out of off-white card.

11 Arrange the envelopes, tags and champagne glass images on the background paper and stick in place. Embellish the page with metal buttons, heart shaped-paperclips and blue vellum hearts.

A simple colour scheme of blue and cream draws the various elements of the scrapbook page together.

The Doorway to Our Future · 49

Girl's Birthday Bliss

Most young girls are desperate to be more grown up, so fulfil their dreams with some shamelessly girly gifts that let them be teenagers for a day. Bringing together fun, fashion and friends, these indulgent interactive items are sure to make the party go with a swing!

A colourful booklet full of photos of all her special friends is a great way to send a girl best wishes on her birthday. Go to town by dressing up the pages with girly stickers, ribbons and funky fibres. All this is kept under wraps in a pretty tin to up the 'wow' factor. Girls will simply adore the party bag, styled like a trendy handbag, with a coordinating tag that hides a dinky notebook. A novel party activity book pictures four fashionably clad teen girls, each cut into three panels, so that the sections can be turned over separately to create a selection of different outfits. The party guests can then spend a blissful afternoon colouring in the pages and comparing the results!

In the Swing The flower-shaped pages of the booklet are decoratively hinged with eyelets so that they can swing apart to let you see all of them at once.

Bags of Fun A strip of paper is folded into a concertina and tucked inside a dainty translucent cover for a little novelty notebook embellishment.

Flipbook Fashion Tuck one of these fun flipbooks inside each party bag for every girl guest, each one personalized with a name tag bearing her initial.

In the Swing

YOU WILL NEED

- **textured card – 5 pastel shades**
- **polka dot patterned papers – white background, blue background**
- **scraps of pastel papers**
- **dark pink inkpad**
- **birthday girl photos**
- **stickers, buttons or other embellishments and metal letter charm**
- **funky fibres**
- **white round shallow tin box with lid**
- **5 pastel-coloured eyelets**
- **circle punches – 5cm (2in), 6cm (2⅜in) (optional) and 1.5cm (⅝in)**
- **sponge dauber or cosmetic sponge**
- **Basic Tool Kit (see page 6)**

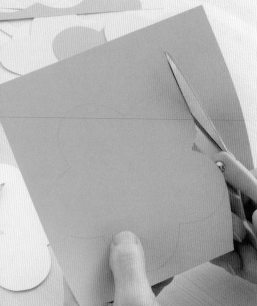

1 Use the template on page 103 to cut a large flower from each of the pastel shades of textured card with scissors. Arrange the flowers in your preferred colour order but with a pink one on top.

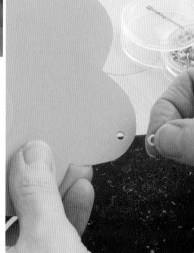

BRIGHT IDEA
You can use paper fasteners (brads), snaps or poppers to create the hinges on the card instead of eyelets.

2 Position the pink flower on top of the second flower. Punch a hole through both layers in the top petal for an eyelet. Insert an eyelet through both holes. Turn the pages face down on the setting mat. Position the setting tool over the back of the eyelet and hit with a hammer to set in place. Tuck the third flower behind the second, punch a hole in the bottom right-hand petal and set an eyelet in place. Continue, alternating the eyelets from top to bottom.

3 Punch or cut a 5cm (2in) circle from one of the polka dot patterned papers. Punch or cut a larger 6cm (2⅜in) circle around the previous circle to create a narrow round frame. Cut two frames from each of the polka dot patterned papers.

4 Print or select suitable photos of the birthday girl and her friends that will fit within the little frames. Draw a pencil line around the frames onto the photos and then cut out slightly inside the line. Stick the frames onto the photos.

5 Open out the booklet and arrange the photo frames on the panels so that some overlap the edges. Stick in place. Decorate the panels with stickers, buttons or other embellishments.

6 Stick one of the punched-out polka dot circles on the front of the booklet. Using a sponge dauber or cosmetic sponge, dab a little dark pink ink around the edge of the cover of the booklet. Tie funky fibres through the top eyelet. Tie a metal letter charm with the first letter of the recipient's name in place with the funky fibres. Tie funky fibres through all the other eyelets to finish.

A big surprise awaits the birthday girl, as the subtle front page gives little indication of the delights in store.

7 If your tin is not white, paint it following Step 1 on page 17. Punch lots of 1.5cm (⅝in) spots from several shades of pastel paper. Stick the spots all over the tin. To finish, use a sponge dauber or cosmetic sponge to dab pink ink around the edge of the tin.

Bags of Fun

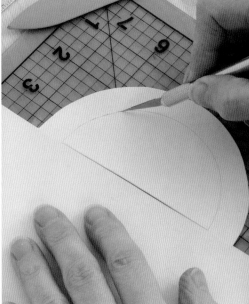

YOU WILL NEED

- pink paper
- scraps of pastel papers
- patterned papers – large checked, large spotted
- pink polypropylene or heavyweight vellum
- pink broad-tip marker pen (optional)
- funky fibres
- metal letter charm
- 1.5cm (⅝in) circle punch
- Basic Tool Kit (see page 6)

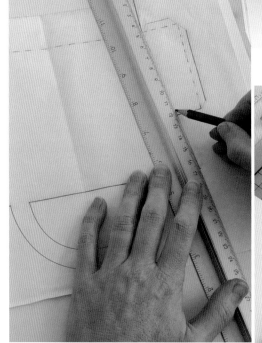

1 Enlarge the bag template on page 103 on a photocopier or computer according to the percentage specified. Trace the template, including the inner details, onto white heavyweight card and cut out. If using ordinary paper to trace, you will see the lines better by holding the template on a window in daylight or on a lightbox. Turn the template around, line up the base of the template with the drawn base and draw the second side of the bag.

2 Cut out along the solid lines using a craft knife. Score the lines indicated by dashed lines on the template. Fold along the scored lines and crease with a bone folder. Open out again.

3 Colour the handle and side panels with a pink broad-tip marker pen or cover with pink paper. Punch lots of 1.5cm (⅝in) spots from the pastel papers and stick all over the bag.

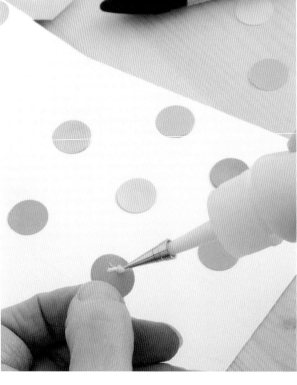

BRIGHT IDEA
If you don't have a circle punch of the right size, draw around a coin onto white paper and colour in with felt-tip pens.

4 Apply glue to the tabs of the bag, fold up and stick in place. Decorate the bag with funky fibres.

BRIGHT IDEA
If you can't find this type of large checked paper, simply cut strips of bright pink paper and fold in the same way.

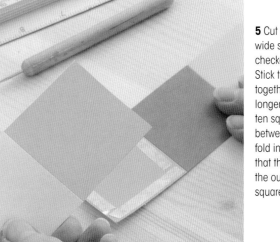

5 Cut two 5cm (2in) wide strips from the large checked patterned paper. Stick the end squares together to make a longer strip with eight or ten squares. Score across between the squares and fold in a concertina so that the colours are on the outside on the last squares of the booklet.

6 Using the template on page 103, cut a small flower from large spotted patterned paper. Punch a 1.5cm (⅝in) circle from pink paper and stick in the centre of the flower. Cut two 6cm (2⅜in) squares of pink polypropylene or heavyweight vellum and stick the flower on one of them.

BRIGHT IDEA
You could invite the older children to decorate their own bags to take home with them after the party is over.

7 Punch a hole in one corner of the squares, then sandwich the paper booklet between the two squares and punch a hole through that too. Tie the booklet and squares together with funky fibres, attach a metal letter charm and tie onto the bag handle.

Flipbook Fashion

YOU WILL NEED

textured card – 5 pastel shades
scraps of lilac card and yellow paper
pink polypropylene or heavyweight vellum
colouring pencils
narrow sheer ribbons
funky fibres
butterfly buttons
metal letter charm
Basic Tool Kit (see page 6)

1 Photocopy or scan the teen girl pictures on page 104 and print out onto white paper, copying one of them twice to use on the front cover. With the girl positioned centrally, trim the first picture to 14cm (5½in) square. Lay tracing paper over the trimmed picture and mark the position of the neck, waist and legs as well as the four corners. Use the tracing to mark the other three pictures in exactly the same way and trim to size.

2 Cut two 15cm (6in) squares of pink textured card and another four squares in other pastel shades. Put the pink card squares to one side and then stick a teen girl picture on each of the other squares using dry adhesive sheets for best results.

3 Mark lines across the first square so that the picture is divided into four sections. The lines go through the neck, waist and mid-calf. Put the pages together in a pile and punch two 3mm (⅛in) holes in the centre of the left-hand side of each marked panel.

4 Use one punched panel as a guide to punch holes in matching position down the left-hand side of the two pink card squares. Put the picture pages together in a pile again and cut along the marked lines.

5 Layer the pages so that the two plain pink ones are on the top and bottom. Tie the book together using narrow sheer ribbons and funky fibres.

BRIGHT IDEA
Tie the pages together quite loosely with the ribbons and funky fibres so that the book can turn freely.

6 Colour in the remaining teen girl picture with colouring pencils and cut out. Stick the figure on the front cover along with the little gift boxes and then embellish with butterfly buttons. Leave the inside pages to be coloured in at the party.

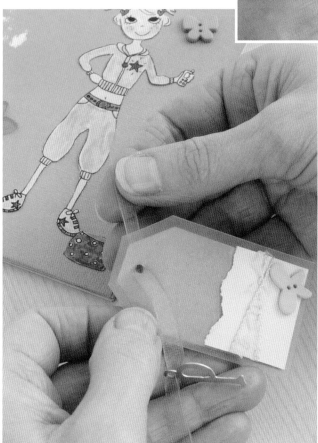

7 Cut a 3.5 x 6cm (1½ x 2⅜in) tag shape from lilac card. Stick onto a piece of pink polypropylene or heavyweight vellum and cut out slightly larger all round. Punch a small hole at the top. Tear a piece of yellow paper to fit the bottom of the tag, wrap with funky fibres and embellish with a butterfly button. Tie a metal letter charm, with the birthday girl's first initial, through the tag hole and attach to the front cover with adhesive foam pads. On other books, add a different initial tag for each guest.

Choose pretty buttons and charms in pastel shades to embellish the tag in suitably girly style.

Boy's Birthday Bonanza

Lads deserve their own special style of birthday celebration, and always appreciate the intriguing and inventive, along with the colourful and exciting. These circus-themed items, with their mesmerizing moving elements, are sure to satisfy their fascination with how things work.

The party invitation card sets the scene in dramatic Big Top style with two performing seals that suddenly pop up above the circus tent. Boys will spend hours satisfying their curiosity as to how the simple mechanism operates, and for extra entertainment value, you could send out the invitations in black and white, allowing each guest to colour in their own. For the party itself, make an amazing all-action hat that features a ball-juggling clown sporting a revolving bow tie! After the party is over, create a memorable page for your scrapbook album using photos from the event and fun interactive elements. The designs could easily be adapted for a pirate party or a fun day at the pool.

Seal Sensation Really grab their attention with this show-stopping circus invite that reveals its star performers when you pull on the end sections of the card.

Head in a Spin Turn the acetate to make the clown juggle the balls, while the ingenious mechanism at the back turns the bow tie in the opposite direction.

Clowning Around When the tab at the bottom of the scrapbook page is pulled, the birthday boy's name is spelled out as the pages flip over.

Seal Sensation

YOU WILL NEED

- white medium textured card
- scraps of blue card
- black fine-line pen
- marker pens – silver, bright colours
- children stickers
- 2 pastel-coloured eyelets
- 2 brightly coloured star-shaped paper fasteners (brads)
- yellow stranded cotton
- Basic Tool Kit (see page 6)

BRIGHT IDEA Get the children involved making the party invitations – they can colour in the motifs ready for cutting out.

1 Transfer two opposite-facing flags and seals and one circus tent motif from page 105 onto white paper. If tracing, mark along all the lines with a fine-line black pen. Colour the seals with a silver marker pen and then colour in the rest of the designs using bright-coloured marker pens. To indicate the interior of the tent, use slightly paler shades.

2 Cut two 25 x 10cm (10 x 4in) pieces of the white textured card. Score one piece 5cm (2in) from the left-hand short side, turn the card over and then score again 8.5cm (3⅜in) from the same short side. Repeat on the second piece of card. Fold both pieces of card in a concertina, with a valley fold nearest to the end of the strip and a mountain fold next.

3 Cut two pieces of white medium card 4.5 x 11cm (1¾ x 4⅜in). Measure 3cm (1¼in) from the bottom right-hand corner along both adjacent edges and score diagonally between the marks on both card pieces. Make a valley fold along the score lines. Apply double-sided tape to both triangles. Stick one tab between the score lines on the reverse side of each piece of the main card, positioning the tab 3mm (⅛in) from the first fold line and so that the bottom edge of the tab is 4.2cm (1⅝in) from the top edge of the card.

4 To join the two pieces of the main card together, apply double-sided tape to the reverse side of the end section on each piece and stick each to the reverse side of the unfolded section of the other piece so that the pop-up tabs are on the inside. Cut out the tent and stick on the front of the card.

5 Cut along the bottom edge of the barrels on the seal motifs and cut around the seals roughly. Stick the seals onto the pop-up tabs so that the barrels are level with the top of the card. Cut carefully around the seals and the balls with small, pointed scissors. Cut out the two flags and stick one on either side of the circus tent. Draw in the flagpoles with a black fine-line pen.

BRIGHT IDEA
Cut away as much of the white border of the stickers as you can for a more professional result.

6 Attach stickers of children on the left-hand side of the card so that they will be hidden when the card is folded up. Punch a small hole in the centre at each end of the card, insert an eyelet into each and set in place (see Step 2, page 52).

7 Cut two small tags from blue card and punch a small hole in each at one end. Write the word 'pull' on one side and decorate the reverse side. Attach the tags through the eyelets at each side of the card with yellow thread, adding a star-shaped paper fastener (brad) to each tag. Write the invitation details on the back of the card.

Pull the two blue tags to make the seals pop up above the circus tent.

Head in a Spin

YOU WILL NEED

- bright blue card 30cm (12in) square
- white self-adhesive Vivelle™
- grey board
- acetate
- scrap of red card
- black fine-line pen (optional)
- marker pens – bright colours
- rubdown letters (optional)
- circle punches – 6mm (¼in) and 1.5cm (⅝in)
- set of compasses
- large paper fasteners (brads) – 1 blue, 1 red
- thin elastic band
- stapler and staples
- Basic Tool Kit (see page 6)

1 Using the template on page 106, cut two clown hat shapes from the bright blue card. To reinforce the front of the hat, cut a strip of medium card 9 x 15cm (3½ x 6in) and stick on the reverse side of one hat shape in the centre. Cut along the curve at the top.

2 Transfer the clown motif on page 106 onto white paper. If tracing, outline with a black fine-line pen. Colour in the clown with marker pens. Cut out and stick on the front of the hat. Colour a piece of white Vivelle™ with a blue marker pen and another piece with a red marker pen and leave to dry. Punch out three 6mm (¼in) spots from the blue-coloured Vivelle™ and two 6mm (¼in) spots from the red-coloured Vivelle™.

3 Using a set of compasses, draw four 3cm (1¼in) circles and four 1.5cm (⅝in) circles on grey board and cut out. Cut two 4cm (1½in) circles and two 2.5cm (1in) circles from white medium card. Punch a hole in centre of each card circle. Stick the circles together to make two cogwheels, with the white card on the outside.

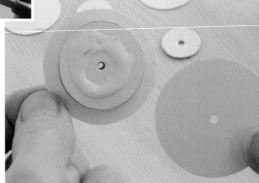

4 Using the set of compasses, draw a 9cm (3½in) circle on acetate and cut out. Colour some white paper using the marker pens, and once dry, punch one or two 1.5cm (⅝in) circles from the different colours to make nine in all. Stick the coloured circles around the edge of the acetate panel. Write or use rubdown letters to create the child's name on some of the circles.

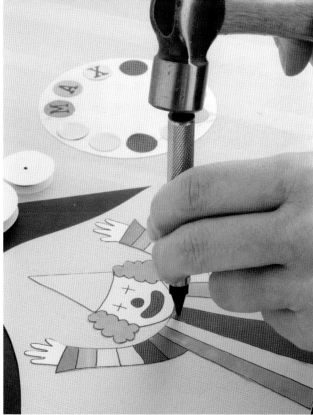

5 Punch a small hole at the top of the clown's hat and another just below his chin. Punch a small hole in the centre of the acetate circle. Using strong glue, stick the large cogwheel in the centre of the acetate circle on the same side as the punched circles. Peel off the backing paper from the Vivelle™ spots and stick onto the clown's top and hat as shown.

BRIGHT IDEA
To make the hat without the moving action, stick the acetate circle with the child's name showing on the inside of the hat.

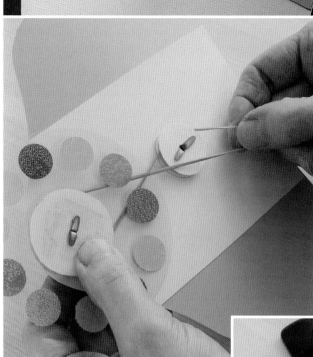

6 Stick red-coloured Vivelle™ onto red card. Using the template on page 106, cut out a bow tie shape and punch a small hole in the centre. Insert the large blue paper fastener (brad) through the bow tie and then into the hole under the clown's chin. Fit the small cogwheel on the back and then open out the paper fastener (brad) at the back.

7 Insert the red paper fastener (brad) through the hole at the top of the clown's hat. Tuck the elastic band around the cogwheel and then fit the acetate circle onto the paper fastener (brad) so that the cogwheel is between the hat and the acetate. Cross the elastic band over and tuck around the small cogwheel. Choose a thin elastic band that will fit snugly around the two cogwheels.

8 Cut a 4cm (1½in) strip of medium to heavyweight card long enough to fit around the child's head. Staple the ends together to create a band. Stick the hat sections on either side of the band so that the ends of the hat are level. Staple the ends so that they stick out.

BRIGHT IDEA
You can simply enlarge or reduce the template to make a clown hat to fit children of different ages or sizes.

Head in a Spin : 63

Clowning Around

YOU WILL NEED

- scrapbook album 30cm (12in) square
- blue textured card 30cm (12in) square
- red and blue self-adhesive Vivelle™
- scraps of bright pastel card
- textured card – purple, orange, pink, blue, yellow
- black fine-line pen
- marker pens – bright colours
- party photos
- bendy shape bar
- circle punches – 6mm (¼in) and 1cm (½in)
- paper fasteners (brads) – blue large round, brightly coloured star-shaped
- Basic Tool Kit (see page 6)

1 Cut a piece of white lightweight card 30cm (12in) square. Measure 19cm (7½in) from the top left-hand corner of the card along both adjacent edges and 17cm (6½in) from the bottom right-hand corner along both adjacent edges. Use a bendy shape bar to draw two curved lines about 1.5cm (⅝in) apart between the marks. Draw a zigzag line between the two curved lines with the black fine-line pen and colour in the triangles with the marker pens. Cut away the quarter circles and lay on the blue textured card.

BRIGHT IDEA
You can simply colour white Vivelle™ with red and blue marker pens (see Step 2, page 62) rather than buying separate colours.

2 Transfer the whole clown image and then the clown's head only on page 106 onto white paper. If you have traced the design, go over the lines with the black pen. Colour in the whole clown with the marker pens and cut out, cutting away the clown's face and hair. Cut the party boy's head out of a photo. Stick the clown body on the blue textured card so that it just tucks under the zigzag border. Stick the zigzag panel in position on the page, then stick the party boy's head and the clown's hat in position.

3 Using the template on page 106, cut out a bow tie shape and punch out three 6mm (¼in) spots from red Vivelle™ for the hat. Punch out three 6mm (¼in) spots from blue Vivelle™ for buttons. Stick the spots on the clown, using the template as a guide to positioning, adding the third red spot to the top of the hat. Punch a small hole under the clown's chin and in the centre of the bow tie. Insert the round paper fastener (brad) through the bow tie and then into the hole under the clown's chin. Punch 1cm (½in) spots from the pastel card scraps and stick in a semicircle between the clown's hands. Colour in the remaining clown head and cut out.

4 For a four-letter name, cut five 5.2 x 6.2cm (2 x 2½in) rectangles from white medium card. Draw five equally spaced lines down each card and colour in with the marker pens. Cut five different-coloured 6 x 7cm (2⅜ x 2⅞in) rectangles from the textured card. Stick each striped card onto a piece of coloured card. Attach the clown's head to the purple panel.

BRIGHT IDEA
If your child's name has more than four letters, simply add additional pages for each extra letter.

5 To make the waterfall mechanism, cut a 31 x 3.5cm (12 x 1⅜in) strip of yellow textured card. Score across the strip 6cm (2⅜in) from one end and then again four times at 2cm (¾in) intervals. Fold the strip along the first four score lines towards the textured side. Sharpen all the folds with a bone folder. Open the strip out again, then fold almost in half along the last 2cm (¾in) score line and sharpen the fold.

6 Stick the blue panel to the first, larger section of the strip so that it butts against the first fold line. Attach the other panels, one after the other, butting against each of the remaining fold lines, finishing with the clown's head panel. Punch out three 6mm (¼in) spots from red Vivelle™ and add to the clown's hat.

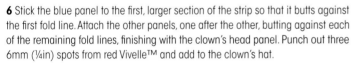

7 Cut a 3.5 x 10cm (1⅜ x 4in) strip of purple card and stick behind the blue panel level with the edge. Punch a small hole at either end of the purple strip, position the waterfall panel on the scrapbook page and punch corresponding holes in the page. Insert a star-shaped paper fastener (brad) into each set of holes to secure the purple strip to the page, leaving the pull tab of the panel underneath free to move. Using a computer, type the letters of the boy's name in black in font size 125 and also the number for the boy's age several times in a range of different bright pastel shades. Print out onto self-adhesive clear printable film.

8 Use a swivel-tip craft knife to cut around the letters and stick one onto each page of the waterfall panel. To finish decorating the page, mat the photos onto the textured card and trim to leave a narrow border. Stick 3.5cm (1⅜in) wide strips of yellow and purple card across the scrapbook page and attach the photos. Cut out the numbers for the boy's age and scatter over the page.

Halloween Horrors

Hallow's Eve, the evening before All Hallows Day, originates from the ancient Celtic festival of Samhain, regarded as a potent time for magic and spirits. Cook up some spellbinding entertainment, featuring bats, witches, black cats and ghosts, with these imaginative ideas.

If you are planning a Halloween party, send some spine-chilling bat invitations, with their lifelike movable components, literally winging out to your guests. No Halloween celebration would be complete without a spell book. This one is made in bright card colours, but you could easily decorate a plain notebook in the same way, with bewitching Halloween papers used to make novelty pop-out frames for fun photos and haunting images, suitably embellished with spooky charms. The hollowed-out, scary-faced pumpkin, originally employed to ward off evil spirits, is another Halloween favourite. Made from traditional honeycomb paper, these 3-D pumpkins are perfect for adding atmosphere to the party room.

Bat-mobile A simple pull mechanism sets the bat's wings in flapping motion for extra impact. Alternatively, just cut out the bat shape and stick it on an invite card.

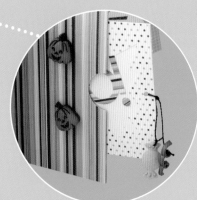

Spellbound A little careful cutting and clever construction is all that is required to make this enchanting album, with its concealed compartments for secret spells.

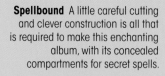

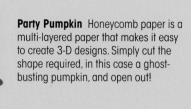

Party Pumpkin Honeycomb paper is a multi-layered paper that makes it easy to create 3-D designs. Simply cut the shape required, in this case a ghost-busting pumpkin, and open out!

Bat-mobile

YOU WILL NEED

- black card
- Halloween patterned papers – spotted, orange checked
- scrap of black self-adhesive Vivelle™
- 2 googly eyes
- Halloween and gift tag stickers
- fine black cord
- set of compasses
- 3 small paper fasteners (brads)
- Basic Tool Kit (see page 6)

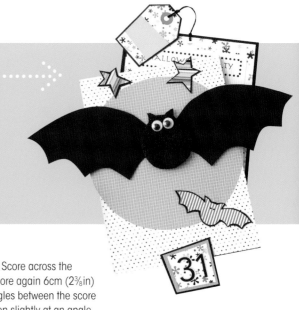

1 Cut a 23 x 16cm (9 x 6¼in) piece of black card. Score across the bottom long side 1cm (½in) from the edge and score again 6cm (2⅜in) in from each short side. Cut out the narrow rectangles between the score lines and the corners, cutting into the centre section slightly at an angle to create a tab. Cut a 2cm (¾in) slot in the centre of the tab score line. Fold along the score lines and sharpen the creases with a bone folder.

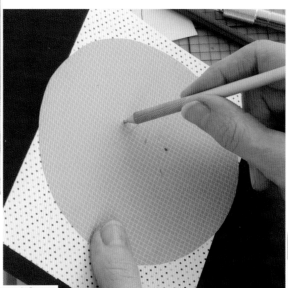

2 Open out the black card and turn over. Cut an 11 x 15cm (4¼ x 6in) piece of spotted Halloween patterned paper and stick on the centre panel. Using a set of compasses, draw a 12cm (4¾in) circle on orange checked Halloween patterned paper, cut out and stick on the centre panel. Trace the slots, holes and centre mark from the template on page 106. Measure 6cm (2⅜in) down from the top edge of the card and put a small cross at that centre point of the card. Line up the cross on the tracing with the cross on the card and then transfer the slot and hole marks. Open out the card and cut the slots, then prick holes where marked with a paper pricker.

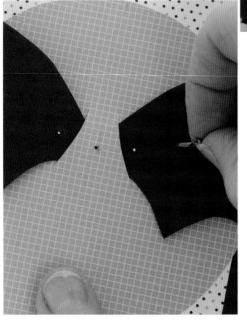

3 Transfer the bat wing shape from page 106 onto black card. Flip the template and draw a second wing. Cut out the wings and prick the two holes at the tab end of each wing where marked on the template.

4 Insert the wings into the slots. On the reverse side, overlap the tabs and line up the end holes. Feed a paper fastener (brad) through both holes and open out. On the right side, line up the remaining wing holes with those on the card and insert paper fasteners (brads). Open out and check that the wings move.

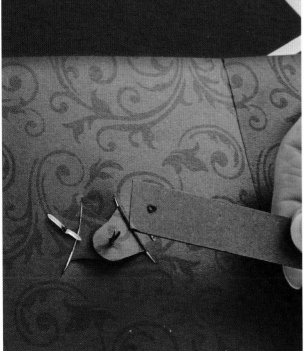

5 Cut two 1.5 x 12cm (⅝ x 4¾in) strips of black card and stick back to back. Prick a hole near one end, open out the central paper fastener (brad) and attach the strip. Feed the end of the strip through the slot at the bottom of the card. Cut a 10.5 x 13cm (4 x 5in) piece of black card and stick double-sided tape across the top and down both sides. Stick over the centre panel of the envelope to cover the mechanism. Apply double-sided tape to the folded-up bottom tab and the edge of the right-hand flap. Fold over the left-hand flap and then fold over the right-hand flap and press to stick. Patterned black card is used here for clarity only, to show the reverse side of the card.

6 Use the template on page 106 to cut a bat body shape from black card. Stick a piece of black Vivelle™ on one side and trim to the same shape. Attach googly eyes using craft glue dots, then stick to the front of the card using adhesive foam pads so that the paper fasteners (brads) are hidden.

7 Stick Halloween stickers such as a date tag, bat and stars, and a gift tag sticker, onto black card and cut out, leaving a narrow border of card all round. Stick the date tag onto the bottom of the black strip so that you are still able to move the wings up and down and trim neatly. Attach the bat and star stickers to the envelope.

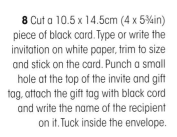

8 Cut a 10.5 x 14.5cm (4 x 5¾in) piece of black card. Type or write the invitation on white paper, trim to size and stick on the card. Punch a small hole at the top of the invite and gift tag, attach the gift tag with black cord and write the name of the recipient on it. Tuck inside the envelope.

BRIGHT IDEA
Vivelle™ is often sold as carpet for dolls' houses. If you can't find it, felt makes a good alternative.

Bat-mobile · 69

Spellbound

YOU WILL NEED

- **orange, black, purple and bright green card**
- **Halloween patterned papers – 5 designs**
- **Halloween photos**
- **Halloween stickers**
- **Halloween tags, tiny buttons and charms**
- **black stranded cotton or no. 5 perlé thread**
- **6mm (¼in) silver-plated jump rings**
- **4 triangular bails (optional)**
- **craft wire (optional)**
- **2cm (¾in) circle paddle punch and hammer**
- **orange large round paper fastener (brad)**
- **Basic Tool Kit (see page 6)**

BRIGHT IDEA
You can alternatively use spray adhesive or dry adhesive sheets to stick the patterned papers to the card rectangles..

1 Cut a 21 x 10cm (8¼ x 4in) rectangle from each card colour, cutting a second orange piece. Score down the centre of each piece widthways and fold. Stick double-sided tape along the fold and top and bottom edges of one orange folded card. Stick the next folded card exactly on top. The outer edges of the pages are left unstuck to create pockets for spells. Repeat until all the pages are stuck together.

2 Cut five 21 x 10cm (8¼ x 4in) rectangles of white medium card and a rectangle the same size from each of the five different Halloween patterned papers. Paint Mod Podge™ onto one piece of white card and stick a piece of Halloween patterned paper on top. Repeat with the other pieces. Smooth each piece down and leave to dry.

3 Score down the centre of each piece widthways and also 5.5cm (2⅛in) from each end. Fold the pieces of card in half with the paper on the outside and sharpen the creases with a bone folder.

4 Mark along the centre fold 2cm (¾in) from the top and bottom edges. Mark out the same distance from the top and bottom edge and 3cm (1⅛in) across from the marks on the fold and join with a pencil to form an upright rectangle. Cut out the rectangular section with a craft knife. Repeat for each piece of card.

5 Decide which aperture panel is going with which colour of card in the spell book. Decorate some of the pages with stickers and others with photos. You can cut out parts of the image rather than sticking rectangular photos on the pages (see Step 6 photo below). Bear in mind that the area for decoration is only halfway out from the centre fold on each double page and the motifs should be fairly central so that you can see them through the aperture.

6 Fold over the side flaps of the aperture cards so that the white card is on the outside and crease with a bone folder. Apply double-sided tape around the edges of both side flaps on each aperture card. Peel off the backing paper and stick your chosen aperture card on each double page of the book, aligning the top, bottom and outside edges.

7 To make spell cards, cut four 9 x 7cm (3½ x 2¾in) pieces of white medium card and four pieces the same size from different Halloween patterned papers. Cut four 7 x 2cm (2¾ x ¾in) strips from different Halloween patterned papers. Cut a fancy edge on each strip using ordinary scissors and stick one to the back of each white card piece, down one short side. Draw a shaped aperture on the rectangles of paper and cut out. Use Mod Podge™ to stick each piece to the front of a white card piece to form a border. Attach a sticker and punch a small hole near the right-hand edge. Tie a tag or button through the hole and then write a spell on the back. On each of the inner pages of the spell book punch a semicircle in the centre of the outside edge using the circle paddle punch and hammer.

BRIGHT IDEA
If you don't have a circle paddle punch, draw a semicircle with a coin and cut out the shape.

8 To make the front cover, cut a 10 x 10.5cm (4 x 4⅛in) piece of orange card and a piece of Halloween patterned paper the same size. Draw a jaggy aperture on the paper, cut out and stick on the card. Punch a small hole in the centre on the right-hand side and insert the large round paper fastener (brad). Stick the decorated card on the front of the book. Tie lots of tiny Halloween buttons down a 65cm (25in) length of black thread. Tie the thread to the paper fastener (brad).

9 Join four or five jump rings together to make a short chain. Attach the chain to the top of a Halloween charm or button. If there is a suitable hole, use a triangular bail, otherwise cut a piece of coloured card the same size as the charm and sandwich a loop of wire or thread between the charm and card shape. Make another three charm chains.

10 Punch a hole with a paper pricker on the fold line at the top of each aperture in the spell book. Open the end jump ring, feed through the hole, then close again. Attach a different Halloween charm to each aperture. Tuck the spell cards into each slot and, if you like, add further stickers to the pages. Close the book, wrap the button thread around several times and loop around the paper fastener (brad) to secure.

If you open the spell book fully, it can be displayed on a shelf or hung as a mobile.

Party Pumpkin

YOU WILL NEED

- bright orange and black card
- orange honeycomb paper
- black no. 8 perlé thread
- tiny Halloween buttons
- black cord or cord elastic
- Basic Tool Kit (see page 6)

BRIGHT IDEA
Make several pumpkins
in the same way and
string them across the
room to create
a garland.

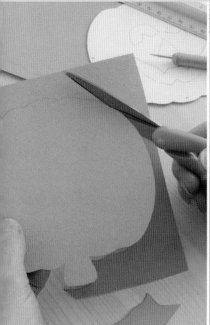

1 Transfer the larger and smaller pumpkin shapes separately on page 106 onto white lightweight card, adding the face features to the larger pumpkin, and cut out around the outlines to make templates. Use the larger template to cut two pumpkins from bright orange card and cut out. Score down the centre of each and fold in half. Sharpen the creases with a bone folder.

2 Lay the smaller pumpkin template on the orange honeycomb paper so that the channels are vertical. Draw around the edge and cut out. Paint Mod Podge™ over one side of the honeycomb shape and stick centrally on one piece of pumpkin-shaped card. Paint Mod Podge™ on the second side of the honeycomb shape and stick the other pumpkin-shaped piece of card on top.

3 Once dry, punch small holes where indicated on the template. Tie the card shapes together through the top and bottom holes with black thread, leaving tails of thread. Attach some tiny Halloween buttons to the bottom thread.

4 Open out the pumpkin and tie the sides together, again leaving tails of thread. Tie tiny Halloween buttons onto the tails of thread. Cut out two sets of face features from black card. Use dry adhesive tape to stick the pieces onto either side of the pumpkin. Tie onto black cord or cord elastic to hang.

Sensational Silver Wedding

The practice of giving a particular present for a wedding anniversary began in medieval Germany, where a silver wreath was the traditional gift to celebrate 25 years. Bring this custom right up to date with these delightfully surprising yet sophisticated silver decorations.

If you know a couple who are about to celebrate their silver wedding anniversary, this contemporary pop-up card will mark the occasion in style. It may look complicated, but the basic card is simple to construct, with the embellishments added afterwards. An unusual Chinese-style concertina album that can be opened from either side is a lovely way to preserve the memories of a wonderful day. Take a nostalgic look back to the original wedding day on one side and then focus on the present-day celebrations on the other. A fun table decoration would make the ideal gift if you have been invited to a celebratory meal. The 'cake' is hollow and can hide a mini bottle of bubbles for blowing about.

Say it with Silver Strips of card have been added inside the pop-up boxes to provide a novel way of attaching attractive silver-embossed decorations.

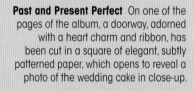

Past and Present Perfect On one of the pages of the album, a doorway, adorned with a heart charm and ribbon, has been cut in a square of elegant, subtly patterned paper, which opens to reveal a photo of the wedding cake in close-up.

Three Tiers for 25 Years Silver foil embellishments are mounted onto coiled and kinked bendy silver wire stems for a finishing flourish to this celebration cake table centrepiece.

Say it with Silver

- off-white scroll patterned card
- silver/grey patterned paper – striped, scroll
- silver self-adhesive foil
- 0.7mm (22swg) silver-plated wire
- 46cm (18in) length of 1.5cm (⅝in) wide silver ribbon
- silver heart charm
- silver cord
- wire cutters (optional)
- round-nosed pliers
- Basic Tool Kit (see page 6)

1 Cut two 20 x 15cm (8 x 6in) pieces of off-white scroll patterned card and score down the centre. Fold in half with the pattern on the inside and sharpen the fold with a bone folder. Put one piece aside for later. On the other piece, mark 6.5cm (2½in) up from the bottom edge on the fold and 5cm (2in) across. Join the marks to make a 5 x 6.5cm (2 x 2½in) box. Cut along the top line and score down from the end of the cut to the bottom edge.

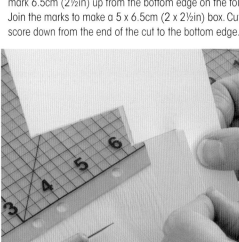

2 Fold the card along the fold line so that the cut section tucks inside the card, then sharpen the crease with a bone folder. Mark 4.5cm (1¾in) up from the bottom edge on this fold and 2.5cm (1in) across. Join the marks to make a 2.5 x 4.5cm (1 x 1¾in) box. Cut along the top line through all the layers and score down from the end of the cut to the bottom edge on both sides of the card. Fold back the boxes on both sides along the score lines. Tuck inside and sharpen the creases as before.

3 Push all three boxes out on the inside of the card. Cut a 1.5cm (⅝in) strip of off-white scroll patterned card. Cut two 10cm (4in) lengths and score across the centre and 1cm (½in) from each end. Stick the strips by the tabs at either end one directly behind the other at the back of the large pop-out box. Cut two 6cm (2⅜in) lengths and score across the centre and 1cm (½in) from each end. Stick one across the back of each small box in the same way.

4 Cut pieces of silver/grey patterned papers to fit the three boxes. Score in half and stick the smaller pieces in place. Cut sections from the large piece to fit around the larger box. Score in half and stick in place. Decorate the boxes with thin strips of off-white scroll patterned card. Stick 2cm (¾in) strips of silver/grey striped patterned paper down each long edge of the card so that 1cm (½in) juts out and trim to size.

5 Apply double-sided tape to the reverse side of the pop-out section of the card and around the outer edge. Remove the inner strips of backing paper altogether and the outer strips part-way. Line up inside the other folded piece of off-white scroll patterned card reserved from Step 1 and stick in place. Pull away the remaining backing paper.

BRIGHT IDEA
To get the best indent effect with the embossing tool, use heavyweight card for covering with the silver self-adhesive foil.

6 Stick silver self-adhesive foil on a 15 x 21cm (6 x 8¼in) piece of white card. Print out the initials and the numbers 2 and 5 on a computer in Textile font in size 100 and use as templates to draw out onto the foil-covered card using an embossing tool. Dab the point of the embossing tool all over the numbers to create a 'beaten metal' texture. Using the template on page 107, draw two hearts on the foil-covered card and decorate with a fine embossing tool. Cut out the initials and numbers.

7 Cut 15cm (6in) lengths of the wire with wire cutters or craft scissors and make a 1cm (½in) coil in one end using round-nosed pliers. Then make several kinks in them to create decorative stems. Attach a letter or number to each of the other ends of wire with strong glue. Use the coil on the end like a decorative paperclip to fix the embellishments to the strips of card inside each box.

8 Use the templates to draw out the numbers onto silver self-adhesive foil and stick on the front of the card. Dab with the embossing tool to texture as before. Cut a 2cm (¾in) wide strip of silver/grey scroll patterned paper. Fold around the finished card so that the ends overlap in the centre at the front and trim. Stick the ends together. Stick a length of silver ribbon around the band and trim. Embellish the strip with a silver heart charm and a silver cord bow.

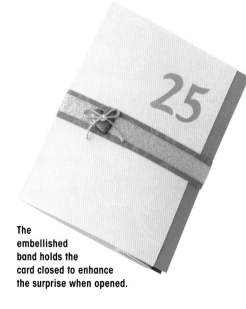

The embellished band holds the card closed to enhance the surprise when opened.

Past and Present Perfect

YOU WILL NEED

- grey board
- plain silver pearlized paper
- silver/grey scroll patterned paper
- white heart patterned vellum
- ivory striped patterned paper
- parchment paper
- silver/grey striped patterned paper
- pale-coloured scroll patterned paper
- silver self-adhesive foil
- grey scroll patterned card
- silver inkpad
- vintage-style stamp
- wedding photos
- wedding memorabilia
- 1.5cm (⅝in) wide silver woven-textured ribbon
- silver organza ribbon
- silver wedding charms
- sponge dauber or cosmetic sponge
- fine sanding pad
- silver sewing thread and needle or sewing machine
- Basic Tool Kit (see page 6)

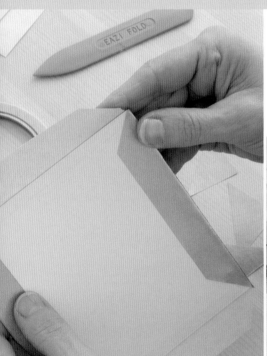

1 For the album covers, cut two 12cm (4¾in) squares of grey board and two 16cm (6¼in) squares of silver pearlized paper. Stick the paper on one side of the board using Mod Podge™ or a dry adhesive sheet. Cut across the corners of the paper 2mm (1/16in) away from the board corners. Fold over the paper along two opposite sides and stick to the board. Tuck under the very edges of the paper at each corner with a bone folder and then stick the remaining sides down.

2 Cut eight 11cm (4¼in) squares of white lightweight card. Lay four of the squares out side by side on a cutting mat. Use the lines on the cutting mat as a guide to apply a strip of double-sided tape across each square 2.5cm (1in) from the top and bottom edges of each piece.

BRIGHT IDEA
If you prefer, you can use spray adhesive to stick the silver paper on the album covers.

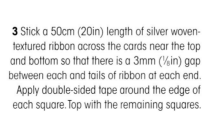

3 Stick a 50cm (20in) length of silver woven-textured ribbon across the cards near the top and bottom so that there is a 3mm (⅛in) gap between each and tails of ribbon at each end. Apply double-sided tape around the edge of each square. Top with the remaining squares.

4 Tuck the prepared album covers under the ribbon at each end so that the white card overlaps the cover by 3mm (⅛in). Stick a piece of double-sided tape across each piece of ribbon to secure to the reverse of the cover and trim. Cut two 11cm (4¼in) pieces of silver/grey scroll patterned paper and stick on the inside of the covers. The album is now ready to decorate. You can view the pages flat or fold up the album concertina fashion and open one side like a book; if you then turn the album round, you can open the other side as though it were a different album.

5 Decorate one side of the album as a memento of your wedding day. To create a 'vintage' memorabilia effect, print out some of your favourite photos in black and white. A scanner and computer are ideal tools to use to reduce the pictures to fit the album. To draw your attention to the centre of the picture, cut a heart out of an 11cm (4¼in) square of white heart patterned vellum and stick over the photo. Embellish the page with tiny silver charms and silver organza ribbon bows.

6 As the album is so small, it is fun to reduce the size of invites, menus or the order of service and include them on the pages. Use the template on page 107 to make an envelope. Stick the envelope onto one of the pages, reduce the invite or other item to fit using a scanner and computer or a photocopier and tuck inside. Attach a silver charm on the flap to weight it down.

BRIGHT IDEA
Use acid-free paper and adhesives for the album if you intend to keep it for many years, to help prevent deterioration.

7 Apply silver ink to a vintage-style stamp and stamp onto one of the pages. Dab silver ink with a sponge dauber or cosmetic sponge around the edge to create a border. Print out a photo such as a close-up of the wedding rings and trim to about 7cm (2¾in) square. Rub the edges of the photo with a fine sanding pad to distress and then stick in the centre of the page. Print or write the date of the wedding on white paper and cut out as a strip. Stick the strip across the corner of the photo.

8 Cut an 11cm (4¼in) square of ivory striped patterned paper. Draw a 6cm (2⅜in) square in the centre and score down the right-hand side. Cut along the other three sides with a craft knife. Open the door and dab silver ink around the edge. Stick a suitable photo, such as a close-up of the wedding cake, on one of the pages of the album and then stick the door frame on top. Attach a charm and ribbon to create a tab for opening.

9 Cut a 20cm (8in) square of parchment paper. Score 5cm (2in) from each edge. Cut out the small squares in each corner and then fold in each side and sharpen the creases with a bone folder. Stick an 11cm (4¼in) square of silver/grey striped patterned paper on one of the pages and stick the folded parchment panel in the centre. Attach a silver key charm to one of the panels so that it still opens out. Fill with a letter, a pressed flower from the bouquet or some other piece of memorabilia.

Make the other side of the album into a celebration of the present-day anniversary. Use coloured contemporary photos and bold patterned papers and vellum as a complete contrast to the wedding day memories. Also include photos of any children or grandchildren for a lasting memento.

10 Reduce a favourite photo from the day, sand the edges to distress and then stick on the back page. Close the book and decorate the front cover. Cut an 11 x 5cm (4¼ x 2in) piece of pale-coloured scroll patterned paper. Tear along the top edge. Sew around the straight edges with silver thread and then dab the edges with silver ink. Cut out the numbers 2 and 5 from silver self-adhesive foil. Stick on the panel and create a texture on the numbers by dabbing with an embossing tool.

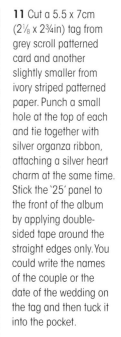

11 Cut a 5.5 x 7cm (2⅛ x 2¾in) tag from grey scroll patterned card and another slightly smaller from ivory striped patterned paper. Punch a small hole at the top of each and tie together with silver organza ribbon, attaching a silver heart charm at the same time. Stick the '25' panel to the front of the album by applying double-sided tape around the straight edges only. You could write the names of the couple or the date of the wedding on the tag and then tuck it into the pocket.

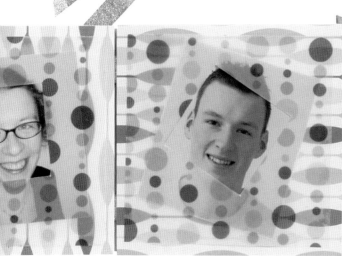

Three Tiers for 25 Years

YOU WILL NEED

- grey board
- silver/grey scroll patterned paper
- silver self-adhesive foil
- white paper texture paint
- white acrylic paint
- 0.7mm (22swg) silver-plated wire
- wedding embellishments
- 1.5cm (⅝in) wide silver ribbon
- set of compasses
- stencilling or other stiff brush
- scallop-edged scissors
- wire cutters (optional)
- round-nosed pliers
- Basic Tool Kit (see page 6)

2 Cut out the hexagon shapes and use the two smaller hexagons to draw a second hexagon inside the largest and the middle-sized hexagon. Cut out the inner hexagons with a craft knife. Cut three strips of grey board, one 5cm (2in), one 3cm (1¼in) and one 2cm (¾in) wide. Measure the length of the sides on the largest hexagon and cut six pieces that size from the 5cm (2in) strip. Repeat for the middle-size hexagon with the 3cm (1¼in) strip and again for the smallest hexagon with the remaining strip.

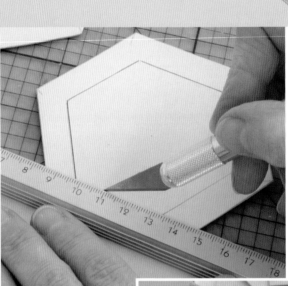

3 Lay the card pieces side by side in a row and join together with a length of double-sided tape along the top and bottom edges. Wrap each strip around the corresponding hexagon to create the sides.

1 Using a set of compasses, draw a 10cm (4in) diameter circle onto grey board. Using the compasses set at the same 5cm (2in) radius, insert the point into the circle, then make a mark on the circle with the pencil end. Move the point to the pencil mark and make another mark. Continue until you return to the first point. Join the pencil marks to make a hexagon. Repeat with circles of 7cm (2¾in) and 4cm (1½in) in diameter.

BRIGHT IDEA
Make sure that you keep the compasses at the exact same setting for drawing the circle and marking the sides of the hexagon.

4 Stick the hexagons one on top of the other to make the tiered cake shape. Tear small pieces of thin white paper and use Mod Podge™ or PVA (white) glue to paste over the joins and edges of the tiers to cover. Continue adding the papier mâché until the cake shape is completely covered in a single layer of paper. Leave to dry.

5 To create the handmade paper look, dab white paper texture paint all over the cake decoration using a stencilling or other stiff brush. Once the texture is even all over, leave to dry. Wash the brush out carefully. Apply a coat of white acrylic paint and leave to dry.

6 Cut three strips of silver/grey scroll patterned paper 3.5cm, 2.5cm and 1.5cm (1⅜in, 1in and ⅝in) wide. Cut along one edge of each piece using scallop-edged scissors. Stick the bands around the cake decoration.

7 Stick silver self-adhesive foil onto a piece of white medium card. Print out the initials and the number 25 on a computer using Textile font in size 100, or draw your own or trace from a magazine. Transfer onto the foil-covered card using an embossing tool. Mark the numbers and letters with the tip of the embossing tool to texture and cut out. Cut out a few balloon shapes from the foil-covered card and use the embossing tool to decorate.

8 Cut 15cm (6in) lengths of the wire with wire cutters or craft scissors. Using round-nosed pliers, coil the wire near one end, leaving a tail, and then kink the wire a few times to create a fancy stem. Bend the coil so that it is perpendicular to the stem. Stick a balloon shape to the end of the wire with strong glue, punch a hole in the first tier of the cake and insert the wire. Bend the tail over on the inside to secure. Add other embellishments in the same way and then stick the initials on the top tier. Stick silver ribbon around the cake to finish.

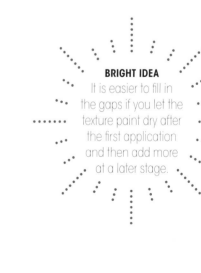

BRIGHT IDEA
It is easier to fill in the gaps if you let the texture paint dry after the first application and then add more at a later stage.

Christmas Crackers

The festive season is the prime time for pop-up papercrafting. To save on precious time nearer the event, get a head start with the earlier-than-ever availability of materials. Then steal the show with these dazzling and dynamic items, as enchanting as they are intriguing.

What better way to count down to the big day than with a fun-packed advent calendar. With 24 days to fill, you have lots of creative ideas here for making a variety of different hiding places for charms and treats, all delightfully dressed up with decorative ribbons, buttons and brads. The calendar can be tied up and safely stored away for next year, when you can ring the changes with some new surprise elements. Whether you send a few cards or dozens at Christmas, it's always nice to make some unique handmade cards for your closest friends and family. This unusual swivel-design card is really simple to make and even folds flat for mailing. Bring some extra-special sparkle to your hallway with a glamorous, glittering 3-D star, again easily accomplished using the template provided.

Twinkle and Twirl The Christmas tree is cut around, leaving the centre scored panel intact, so that the card can be folded to create the swivel effect. You could change the motif to a snowman, Christmas pudding or star.

Star Attraction The inner layers of this stunning Christmas decoration are supported, as well as enriched, by fine red glitter thread and eye-catching red beads.

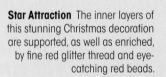

Countdown Encounters An assortment of enticing pockets, flaps and file folders are created to hold a host of mini surprises in this concertina-style advent calendar.

Twinkle and Twirl

YOU WILL NEED

- cream card
- glitter self-adhesive foil – green, red, gold
- scraps of lime green and bright red card
- pale green card
- dual-tip pale green marker pen
- 6mm (¼in) circle punch
- star paddle punch (optional)
- Basic Tool Kit (see page 6)

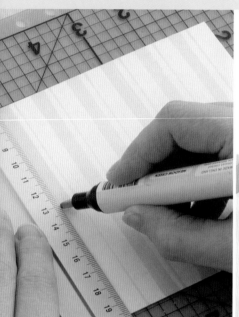

1 Cut a piece of cream card 20 x 13cm (8 x 5in). Lay the card on a cutting mat or graph paper so that the card is lined up with the grid. Using the grid lines as a guide, draw vertical thin green lines with the marker pen on the card at regular intervals. Using the broad tip end of the pen, draw wider lines in between. Trim the card slightly along the top and bottom edges to neaten the stripes.

2 Transfer the Christmas tree and pot motifs on page 107 to the reverse side of the green and red glitter self-adhesive foil. Cut out, peel off the backing paper and stick down in the centre of the card. Mark 8.5cm (3¼in) in from each side along the top and bottom edges. Score vertically to join each set of marks, but without scoring through the tree. Using a craft knife, cut from the score lines at the top around the tree to the score lines at the bottom.

3 Punch 6mm (¼in) circles from the red and gold glitter self-adhesive foil, remove the backing paper and stick all over the tree. Punch or cut out a gold star that will fit between the score lines and stick at the top of the tree.

4 Swivel the card along the fold lines to hide the sparkly side of the tree. Cut a piece of lime green card to fit in the cutout of the folded card. Draw around the left-hand side of the tree onto the card and cut along the lines. Position the lime green card and draw the right-hand side of the tree. Cut out the lime green tree and stick in place. Cut small parcel shapes from lime green and bright red card. Decorate with thin strips of glitter self-adhesive foil and stick along the bottom of the card.

Star Attraction

YOU WILL NEED

- **glitter self-adhesive foil – red, gold**
- **red card with a red core**
- **fine red glitter thread**
- **red beads**
- **narrow red ribbon**
- **sewing needle**
- **Basic Tool Kit (see page 6)**

BRIGHT IDEA
Using card that is
red all the way through
gives a better finish to the
decoration, as there will be
no white visible along
the cut edges.

1 Peel off the backing paper from the red glitter self-adhesive foil and stick the sheet on one side of the red card. Turn the card over and stick the gold glitter self-adhesive foil on the reverse side.

2 Transfer the star template on page 108 onto white paper – it fits onto a sheet of A4 (US letter) paper. Tape the template onto one side of the foil-covered card.

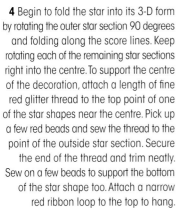

4 Begin to fold the star into its 3-D form by rotating the outer star section 90 degrees and folding along the score lines. Keep rotating each of the remaining star sections right into the centre. To support the centre of the decoration, attach a length of fine red glitter thread to the top point of one of the star shapes near the centre. Pick up a few red beads and sew the thread to the point of the outside star section. Secure the end of the thread and trim neatly. Sew on a few beads to support the bottom of the star shape too. Attach a narrow red ribbon loop to the top to hang.

3 Using a metal safety ruler and craft knife fitted with a new blade, cut along all the solid lines inside the star shape. Once the inner lines are all cut, check that all the sections are cut properly, then cut around the outline to cut the shape out. Score along the short dashed lines as indicated on the template.

Countdown Encounters

YOU WILL NEED

- grey board
- cream hammer-effect paper
- large sheet of cream heavyweight hammer-effect card
- red, green and cream lightweight card
- red, green and white vellum
- selection of Christmas patterned papers
- meadow green dual-tip marker pen
- Christmas photos
- red and green rickrack braid
- Christmas charms and stickers
- Christmas ribbon, and funky fibres (optional)
- red and green photo tabs
- metal and rubdown or sticker numbers
- die-cut alphabet set (optional)
- set of compasses
- paper fasteners (brads) – red, green, white small star-shaped; red, green small round
- red, green and white sewing thread and sewing machine
- red and green stranded cotton and sewing needle
- punches – buttonhole, 1cm (½in) circle, mini-envelope (optional)
- mini-envelope template sheet
- vellum adhesive (optional)
- stapler and staples
- Basic Tool Kit (see page 6)

1 To make the end panels, cut two pieces of grey board 10 x 24cm (4⅛ x 9¾in) and two pieces of cream hammer-effect paper 12 x 26cm (4¾ x 10¼in). Draw vertical stripes onto the paper with the marker pen (see Step 1, page 86). Stick the reverse side of the paper onto one side of the board using Mod Podge™ or a dry adhesive sheet. Cut across the corners of the paper 2mm (¹⁄₁₆in) away from the board corners. Fold over the paper along the two long sides and stick to the board. Tuck under the very edges of the paper at each corner with a bone folder, then stick the short sides down.

BRIGHT IDEA
The card folds better if you score valley folds on the right side and mountain folds on the reverse side.

2 Cut two pieces of cream hammer-effect card 27.5 x 24cm (11 x 9¾in) and a narrow strip 24 x 2cm (9¾ x ¾in). Mark along the top and bottom edges of the large card pieces 6cm (2⅜in) from the left-hand side, then a further 12cm (4¾in) to leave a panel 9.5cm (3⅞in) at the other end. Score down the card to join these sets of marks on one side. Turn each card piece over and score 12cm (4¾in) again from the left-hand side. Fold the panels along the score lines to create a concertina.

3 Score the strip lengthways down the centre and fold in half. Lay down as a mountain fold and stick double-sided tape along the two edges. Remove the backing tape and butt the side edge of the 6cm (2⅜in) panel from each piece of card up to the score line of the strip. Draw green stripes onto the cream card with the marker pen (see Step 1, page 86).

(see Step 1, page 86).

BRIGHT IDEA
Sketch out a plan of your advent calendar before you begin making the various pockets, flaps and file folders.

4 Cut six 8.5 x 8cm (3½ x 3¼in) pieces of red card and six of green card. On two green card panels and one red, attach a piece of red or green rickrack braid at an angle with a little dry adhesive tape at each end. Insert contrasting-coloured star-shaped paper fasteners (brads) to secure. Cut a 6.5 x 4cm (2½ x 1½in) tag from green, red and cream card. Punch a small hole at the top. Attach a Christmas charm to the reverse side as you tie ribbon or funky fibres through the tag hole.

5 Using a set of compasses, draw three pairs of 6cm (2⅜in) circles onto red, green and white vellum and cut out. To create a flap, score a line across the top third of each pair of circles, placed one on top of the other, and cut off the scored section of the top circle of each pair. Machine stitch around the curved edge up to the flap using matching thread. Insert a small star-shaped paper fastener (brad) in the flap. Attach the pockets to the contrasting-coloured card panels using a star-shaped paper fastener (brad) at each side at the end of the stitching.

BRIGHT IDEA
If hand sewing, prick the holes first with a paper pricker and then sew for a neater finish.

6 Cut a 6cm (2⅜in) square from red, green and cream Christmas patterned papers. Score diagonally across the centre. Punch two sets of buttonholes along the edge of red, green and cream card. Hold the 1cm (½in) circle punch upside down and position the holes in the centre. Punch two buttons in each colour. Use red or green stranded cotton to sew one button onto the corner of each triangle and a matching button to the top left-hand corner of a red or green card panel, tying the thread in a knot. Decorate the inside of each square with a little note or a picture, then fold up and wind the cotton around the button on the card.

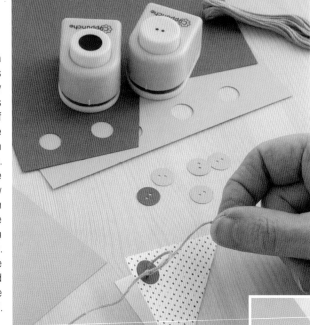

BRIGHT IDEA
You can use real red and green buttons rather than punched card buttons if you prefer.

7 Begin to stick the panels onto the concertina. Use the main picture on page 88 as a guide to see where to position the prepared panels. Remember to apply glue or double-sided tape only across part of the cards that jut out over the edge.

8 Using the template on page 107, cut three file folders from red, green and cream card. Score down the centre and fold in half. Decorate the inside of the files and then stick in position between the red and green panels as shown. Attach a photo tab above each file using a round paper fastener (brad) and swivel to hold the flap closed.

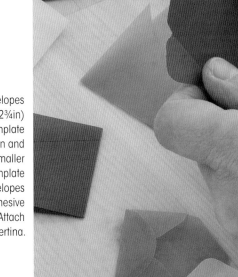

BRIGHT IDEA
You can colour photo tabs with a permanent marker pen to match the advent calendar.

9 Cut three large envelopes about 5 x 7cm (2 x 2¾in) using a mini-envelope template sheet from red, green and white vellum. Cut three smaller envelopes using a template or punch. Stick the envelopes together using dry adhesive tape or vellum adhesive. Attach the envelopes to the concertina.

10 To make the little matchbooks, cut 5 x 14cm (2 x 5½in) strips from green and red card. Score at 1.5cm, 6.5cm and 5mm (⅝in, 2½in and ¼in) intervals. Fold along the score lines and insert staples along the bottom fold line. Decorate the inside of the matchbooks with stickers, drawings or little notes.

BRIGHT IDEA
Make the advent calendar really personal with family photos under some of the flaps.

11 Cut 5 x 10cm (2 x 4in) rectangles from red, green and white vellum. Punch a semicircle in the centre of one short side and then fold in half. Stitch down the sides with matching thread. Stick on the remaining gaps in the concertina panel. To tie the advent calendar, attach a length of green narrow ribbon to the front panel and red ribbon to the back panel. Stick the prepared board end panels in position and use the ribbon to tie around the calendar and store from year to year.

12 Collect together a selection of different numbers. Use metal numbers, rubdowns or stickers. If you have a die-cut alphabet set, cut the numbers from Christmas patterned papers. You can also print out numbers from a computer onto paper or a self-adhesive clear printable film to create your own see-through stickers. Attach the numbers in a random fashion across the advent calendar.

Coordinating Christmas papers, stickers and ribbon add the finishing touches.

13 Stick little photos of your children or fun Christmas stickers behind the flaps on the matchbooks and file folders. Fill the pockets with little knick-knacks or Christmas charms, or little notes saying where a chocolate or other treat is hidden around the house. Decorate the front and back panels of the advent calendar. You can cut out a Christmas tree from glitter self-adhesive foil using the template on page 107, as shown on page 86.

Card Gallery

This collection of cards shows how easy it is to adapt the pop-up techniques used in the projects for different occasions. You can use the step-by-step photos from the main cards to help make these additional designs.

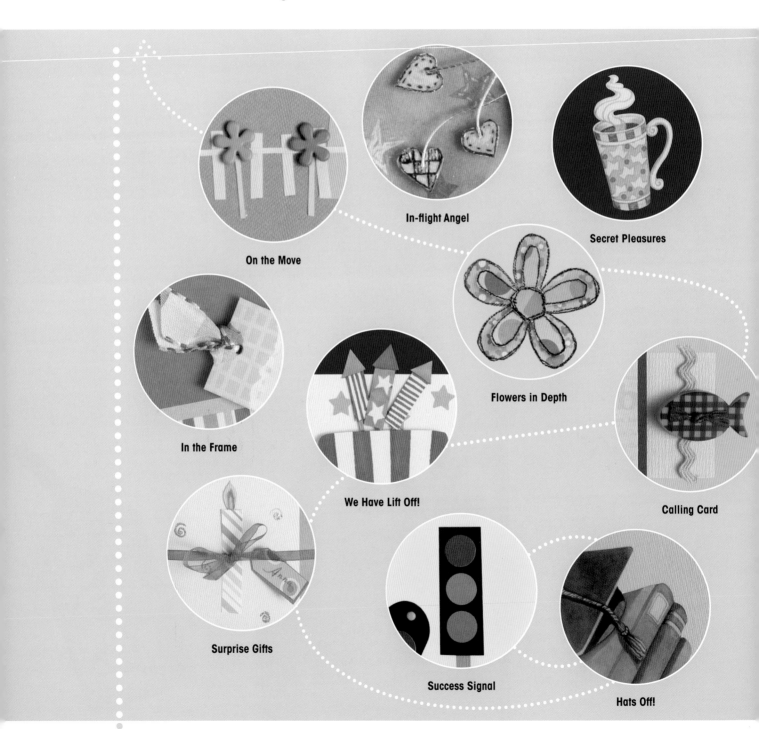

On the Move

In-flight Angel

Secret Pleasures

In the Frame

We Have Lift Off!

Flowers in Depth

Calling Card

Surprise Gifts

Success Signal

Hats Off!

On the Move

This vibrant 'new home' card features the same swivel pop-out element used in the Twinkle and Twirl Christmas card on page 86. It could also be applied to a heart, a snowman or even a box of chocolates.

1 Transfer the main elements of the house on page 109 to the appropriate papers as shown and cut out. Cut a 21.5 x 14cm (8½ x 5½in) piece of purple textured card. Follow Step 2 of Twinkle and Twirl on page 86 to make the card, marking out from the centre line 1.5cm (⅝in) for the score lines.

2 Cut out the details for the house and trees from bright pastel papers and stick onto the card as shown. Cut thin strips of lilac paper to make the fence and stick onto the card.

3 Add very narrow strips of green paper for the flower stems. Bend the metal lugs to break them off flower-shaped paper fasteners (brads) and attach to the stems with adhesive foam pads.

4 Fold the card along the score lines to make the chimney pot come forward and the house swivel out. Use stickers or stamps to write 'Welcome to Your New Home' or 'We're Moving' on the reverse side.

In-flight Angel

The moving mechanism used for the bat wings in the Bat-mobile Halloween card on pages 68–69 has been applied to this dainty Christmas angel. If you can't find an angel stamp, draw a simple angel onto white paper and colour in.

1 Follow Step 1 of the Bat-mobile card on page 68 to cut an envelope from dark blue textured card. Cut a piece of blue star patterned paper slightly smaller than the centre panel and stick in place. Measure 6cm (2⅜in) down from the top edge and put a small cross in the centre at that point. Transfer the slots from the template on page 109 and cut with the envelope open.

2 Stamp an angel with black ink onto white card and heat emboss with clear embossing powder. Cut the angel and hearts out separately. Transfer two wings and one star from page 109 onto white lightweight card. Colour all the pieces to match with colouring pens. Feed the wing tabs into the slots and cross over. Feed a paper fastener (brad) through the cross and first holes on each wing tab.

3 Cut two 1.2 x 15cm (½ x 6in) strips of lilac polypropylene. Prick a hole at one end. Attach one to each end of the wing tabs. Tuck the ends through the slot at the bottom of the card. Stick together with a craft glue dot. Stick the star over the join so that the wings are able to move.

4 Attach the angel to the card front with adhesive foam pads, leaving the area of the wings clear so that the wings can move. Attach the hearts with adhesive foam pads and then stick on pieces of fine silver cord to attach to the angel. Assemble the envelope and make an insert following Steps 5 and 8 on page 69.

Calling Card

This delightful baby card, ideal for a christening, features the same 'waterfall' mechanism as in Clowning Around on pages 64–65 to spell out the baby's name.

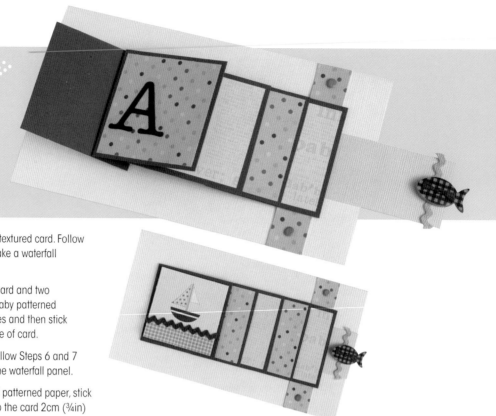

1 Cut an 18 x 20cm (7 x 8in) piece of white textured card. Follow Step 5 of Clowning Around on page 65 to make a waterfall mechanism from pale blue card.

2 Cut five 6cm (2⅜in) squares of dark blue card and two 5.5cm (2¼in) squares of both spotted and baby patterned papers. Stick the papers onto the card squares and then stick a boat embellishment on the remaining piece of card.

3 Beginning with a baby patterned square, follow Steps 6 and 7 on page 65 to assemble and add letters to the waterfall panel.

4 Cut a 1.8 x 10cm (¾ x 4in) strip of spotted patterned paper, stick onto pale blue card and trim to size. Attach to the card 2cm (¾in) from the right-hand side of the card with a blue paper fastener (brad) top and bottom. Stick the end square of the waterfall panel onto the spotted patterned strip and then tuck the pull tab under the strip. Decorate the end of the pull tab with pale blue rickrack braid and a fish button.

Flowers in Depth

This get well card is similar to Say it with Silver on pages 76–77, where slits are cut perpendicular to the fold line. On this card, more slits are cut to create the stems of the flowers.

1 Cut a 14 x 21cm (5⅝ x 8¼in) piece of white lightweight card and score across the centre. Mark across the score line at 1cm and 1.5cm (⅜ and ⅝in) intervals all the way along. Make the same marks 2cm (¾in) lower down. Using the pencil marks as a guide, cut 2cm (¾in) above and below the score line at the first two marks, then 3cm (1⅛in), 2cm (¾in), 4cm (1½in) and finally 2.5cm (1in) above and below the score line for the last pair.

2 Score between the ends of the cut lines, push up the 1cm (½in) wide tabs and fold up the card. Cut a 1cm (⅜in) wide strip of lime textured card. Cut pieces to fit the front of the tabs to make the flower stems and stick in place.

3 Stamp flowers in black ink onto a variety of papers and emboss with clear embossing powder and a craft heat tool. Cut out the separate parts as shown and assemble with glue. Stick on flowers at various heights. Cut small pieces of 'grass' and stick at the base of each flower stem.

4 Decorate the card with strips of flower patterned paper, lime rickrack braid and purple buttons. Use double-sided tape to stick into a 15 x 25cm (6 x 10in) purple textured outer card. Cut a 2cm (¾in) strip of the lime card and fold around the card. Cut a thinner strip of flower patterned paper and stick on top. Cover the join on the band with a stamped flower.

Secret Pleasures

This entertaining retirement card, which slides apart to reveal an inner image, works on the same principle as the tag in the Father's Day project, Best-dressed Bottle, on pages 38–39, except that it is much bigger! Change the concealed motif to suit the recipient.

1 Cut two 10.5 x 7.5cm (4⅛ x 3in) pieces of grey board. Cut several 6mm (¼in) wide strips from an A4 (US letter) sheet of grey board. Stick down the short sides of the grey board pieces and then stick another length across the top of one and the bottom of the other. Cut four 6mm (¼in) squares and stick at the bottom of the side strips to form stop tabs.

2 Cut an 8.5 x 12.5cm (3⅜ x 5in) piece of grey board. Draw a line 6mm (¼in) from each long side and the same distance from the top and bottom edges. Cut out the narrow side strips to create the slider bar. Cut a piece of soft blue textured paper to fit the centre panel.

3 Tuck each end of the slider bar inside one of the prepared grey board panels, apply glue to the thin strips of grey board on three sides and then stick two 10.5 x 7.5cm (4⅛ x 3in) pieces of white ribbed card on top. Dab the edges with blue ink.

4 Attach the dressing gown and other retirement stickers on the front of the closed card. Cut carefully along the centre slot with a craft knife.

5 Decorate the card with golf bag stickers and punctuation marks. Prick two small holes at the top. Thread through fine raffia or cord, tie knots at the front and trim the ends.

We Have Lift Off!

This Fourth of July card features the same pop-up mechanism as in A Slice of Love on pages 44–45, where the flag is 'waved' to launch a battery of fireworks from the hat. It can be easily adapted to celebrate Bonfire Night or New Year.

1 Cut a 20 x 17cm (8 x 6¾in) piece of white textured card, score down the centre and fold in half. Trace the hat, flag, strip (twice) and fireworks (as one piece) on page 109 onto white lightweight card using light pencil marks. Colour the hat, flag and fireworks as shown and cut out.

2 Stick the firework sticks at the top of one card strip. Stick the other strip on the front to strengthen. Cut the slot on the hat and prick the holes where marked. Insert the flag section through the slot and assemble the pop-up mechanism using small paper fasteners (brads).

3 Cut a 6.5 x 10cm (2½ x 4in) piece of blue textured card and attach adhesive foam pads down the sides and along the bottom edge. Stick on the front of the card. Apply thin strips of adhesive foam pad down the sides of the hat and then at the edge of the brim only, making sure that the adhesive foam strips don't obstruct the fireworks and pop-up mechanism.

4 Stick the hat on the front of the card, applying a little glue where it overlaps the blue card panel. Decorate the front of the card with small stars punched from red, white and blue textured card.

In the Frame

This engagement card uses a similar style of envelope to Bat-mobile on pages 68–69 to house a decorative insert, which lifts out to reveal the happy couple romantically framed. Adapt it for Valentine's Day by omitting one of the photos and putting a question mark instead.

1 Follow Step 1 of Bat-mobile on page 68 to cut an envelope from white medium card. Cut a piece of pink patterned paper so that the border runs along the bottom and stick to the front.

2 Using the template on page 109, draw two hearts on the envelope front. Open the envelope out and cut out the hearts. Crop the photos to fit behind the cutouts. Stick on the inside. Punch a semicircle in the centre top edge of the front panel. Follow Step 5 on page 69 to assemble the envelope.

3 Cut a 3 x 6.5cm (1⅛ x 2½in) and a 10 x 14.5cm (4 x 5¾in) rectangle from polka dot patterned card. Punch a hole at the top of the large rectangle and thread ribbon through. Write or print on the back and insert into the envelope.

4 Print or write the couple's name onto vellum. Stick on the front of the polka dot tag. Tear a small piece of green patterned paper and stick to the tag top. Punch a hole and thread ribbon through. Attach to the card front with adhesive foam pads.

Surprise Gifts

Based on the same design as the Say it with Silver card on pages 76–77, this coming-of-age card opens up to present a suitably adorned stack of gift boxes. It can be used for any birthday celebration – just change the numbers on the inside of the card!

1 Make the pop-up and main card from pale blue textured card following Steps 1–3 of Say it with Silver on page 76. Decorate the boxes with patterned papers and assemble the card as shown, following Steps 4–5 on pages 76–77.

2 Decorate the background with swirls of blue and orange pen. Draw swirls of PVA (white) glue over the top, sprinkle on silver glitter and tip off the excess. Leave to dry. Print 1 and 8 in orange on a computer using Techno font at size 200 onto self-adhesive clear printable film and stick onto white card. Add a 1cm (½in) square tab to the bottom of each number and cut out using a craft knife.

3 Cut four 1 x 6cm (½ x 2⅜in) strips diagonally from striped patterned paper and stick onto white card for candles. Draw a flame on each candle and cut out. Stick the candles and numbers on the card strips inside the boxes.

4 Decorate the front of the card with a large candle and swirls in blue and orange pen. Make a small tag from orange textured card and spot patterned paper. Use rubdown letters or write the name of the recipient on the tag and punch a hole at the top. Attach sheer orange ribbon to the back of the card. Thread on the tag and tie in a bow to close.

Success Signal

This fun design features a pop-up tab similar to those used in the Seal Sensation invitation card on pages 60–61, this time to swing up a learner driver's sign into view. It is simple enough to be adapted for all sorts of occasions.

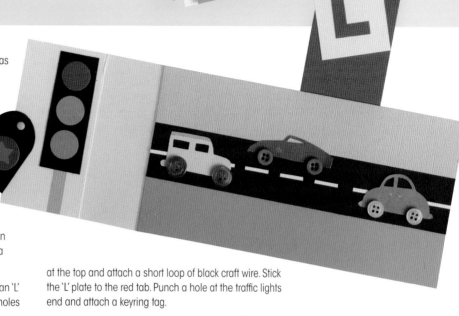

1 Follow Steps 2–3 of Seal Sensation on page 60 to make the main card, but attach only one pop-up strip in red card as shown, or keep the second pop-up tab and write the words 'You've passed!' on it. Stick strips of blue, green and black card on the front of the card and attach thin strips of white paper for the road markings.

2 Using the templates on page 108, cut the cars from coloured card with scissors, then cut out the windows with a craft knife. Colour with a silver pen and stick on the road. Stick small buttons on the cars for tyres.

3 Cut a 2 x 6.5cm (¾ x 2½in) piece of black card. Punch three 1.5cm (⅝in) circles from red, orange and green card and stick on the black card. Stick on the end flap with a blue pole so that it is hidden when the card is closed.

4 Cut out a 2cm (¾in) square of red card and cut to make an 'L' shape. Stick on a 4cm (1½in) square of white card. Punch holes at the top and attach a short loop of black craft wire. Stick the 'L' plate to the red tab. Punch a hole at the traffic lights end and attach a keyring tag.

Hats Off!

This suitably studious-looking graduation card has a simple but effective pop-out section inside, similar to Card with a Catch on pages 36–37, this time featuring a cutout mortarboard.

1 Cut a 21 x 12cm (8¼ x 4¾in) piece of white medium card and cover with graduation hats patterned paper. Follow Step 4 of Card with a Catch on page 37 to score and fold the card.

2 Cut a 22 x 13cm (8¾ x 5¼in) piece of yellow textured card and round the corners with a corner punch. Score down the centre and fold in half. Stick the pop-out card inside. Cut one of the larger graduation hat motifs out roughly and stick onto white card. Cut out around the edge and stick on the right-hand side of the pop-out 'v' shape.

3 To decorate the outside of the card, cut a 16 x 3.5cm (6¼ x 1⅜in) strip of red card. Score across the card 11cm (4¼in) from one end and stick this larger section across the back of the card.

4 Round off the corners of the other end of the strip and attach adhesive hook and loop pads to secure it to the card front. Decorate the card front with graduation and star stickers. Use stickers or rubdown letters to write 'Congratulations' or 'Well Done' on the inside of the card.

Templates

Using the templates

Most of the templates are printed full size, but some need to be enlarged according to the percentage specified. Simply key the percentage into a photocopier or use a photo-manipulation computer program to increase the size by the correct amount.

COPYING

If you have access to a computer and scanner at home, this is the quickest way to copy the templates. Once scanned into a computer program, you can print the template out while saving the image for future use. Print onto lightweight card if you want a more substantial template for drawing around. Alternatively, photocopy the pages you require.

Some of the templates are designs that can be coloured in. To save time tracing and outlining with a black pen, photocopy or print out the motifs onto paper. Print out extra copies in case of mistakes or if you are making several cards.

TRACING

This is the traditional method for copying templates, used before computers and photocopiers were invented – easy and accurate, but a little time-consuming.

1 Lay tracing paper over the template and hold steady or secure with low-tack tape. Trace along the lines with a sharp pencil as accurately as possible.

2 Turn the tracing over onto scrap paper and scribble over the lines on the reverse side using a soft (B) pencil.

3 Place the tracing right side up where you want to transfer the design and draw over the lines with a sharp pencil. Lift off the paper and, if necessary, draw over the lines with a pencil or black fine-line pen.

Building for the Future
pages 12–13

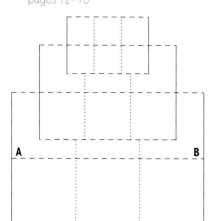

Pop-up Insert
Enlarge at 200%

A   B

Charmed Life
pages 14–16

Pram

Pop-out Posy
pages 20–21

Pop-up Insert

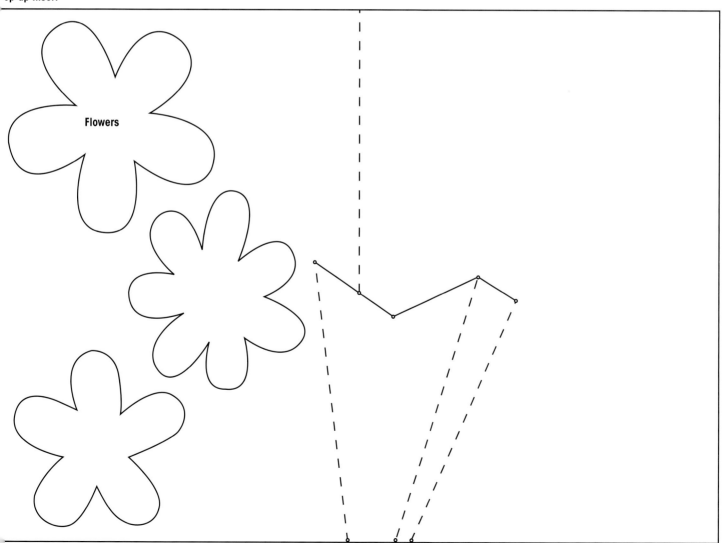

Flowers

Bags of Love
pages 24–25

Small Handbag
Enlarge at 200%

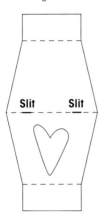

Slit   **Slit**

Large Handbag
Enlarge at 200%

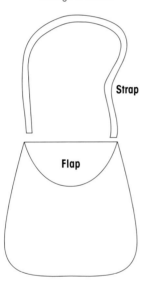

Strap

Flap

Eggsplosion!
pages 28–29

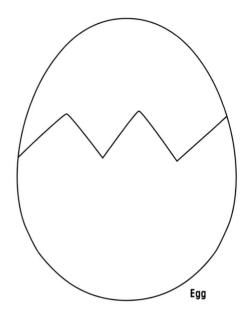

Egg

Chick

'Spring' Flowers
pages 32–33

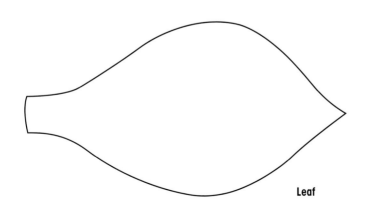

Leaf

Hatch Box
pages 30–31

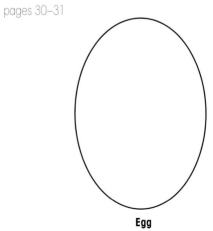

Egg

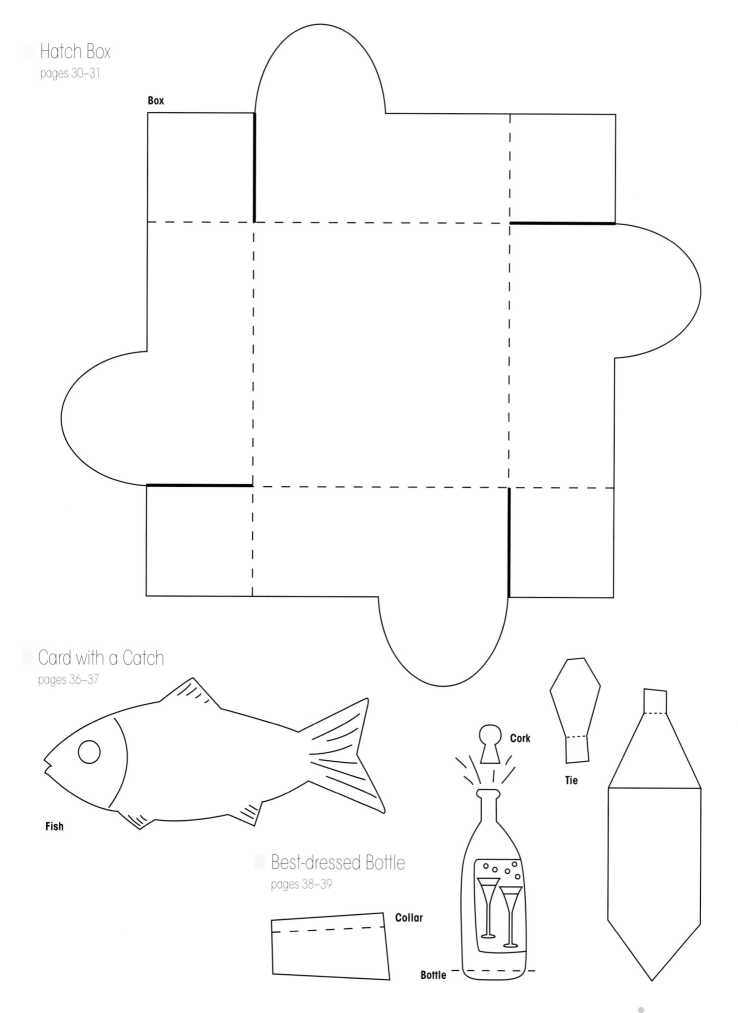

Hatch Box
pages 30–31

Box

Card with a Catch
pages 36–37

Fish

Cork

Tie

Best-dressed Bottle
pages 38–39

Collar

Bottle

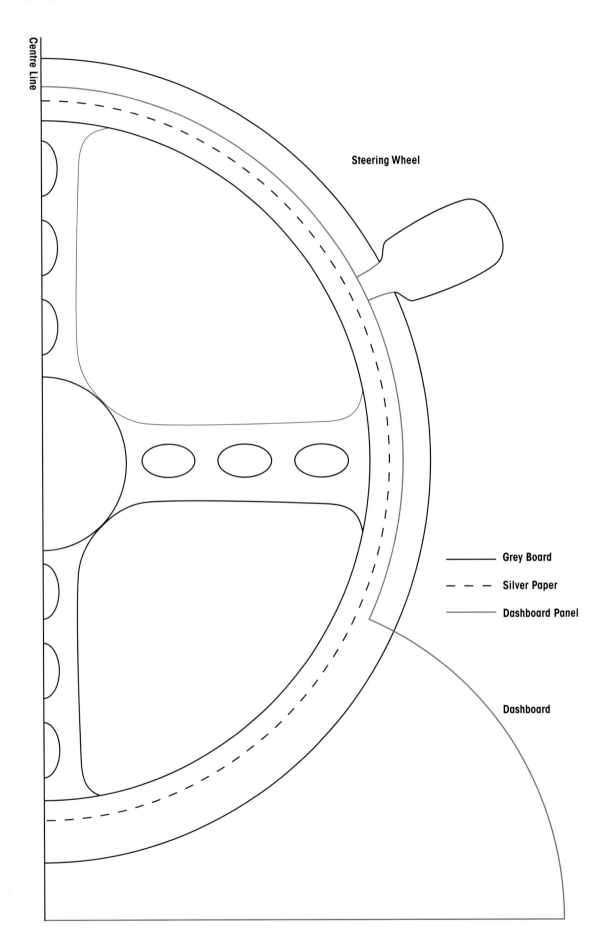

Centre Line

Steering Wheel

———— Grey Board

– – – – Silver Paper

———— Dashboard Panel

Dashboard

Do Me a Favour
page 46

Favours Box
Enlarge at 200%

In the Swing
pages 52–53

Large Flower

Small Flower

Bags of Fun
pages 54–55

Enlarge at 200%

Bag

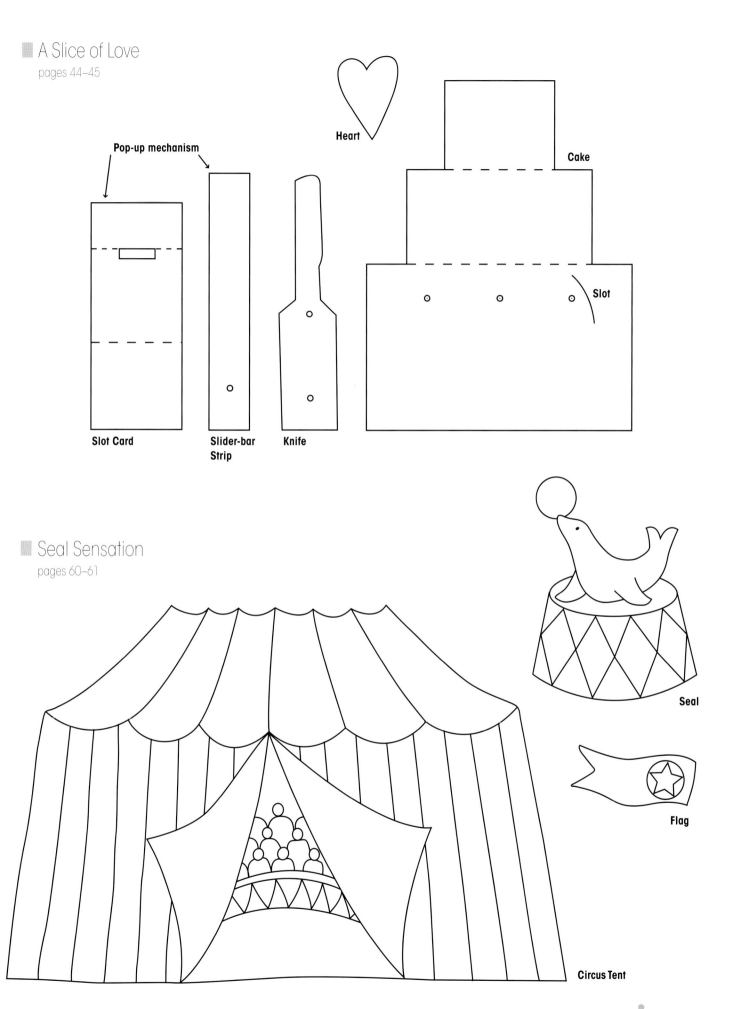

A Slice of Love
pages 44–45

Pop-up mechanism

Heart

Cake

Slot

Slot Card

Slider-bar Strip

Knife

Seal Sensation
pages 60–61

Seal

Flag

Circus Tent

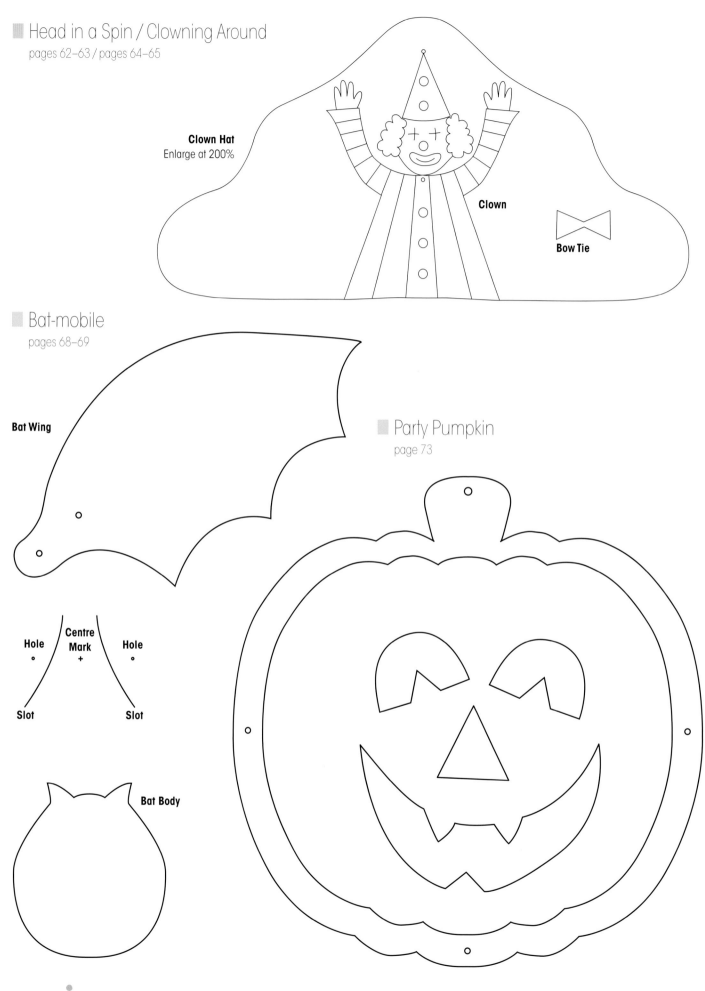

Head in a Spin / Clowning Around
pages 62–63 / pages 64–65

Clown Hat
Enlarge at 200%

Clown

Bow Tie

Bat-mobile
pages 68–69

Bat Wing

Party Pumpkin
page 73

Hole

Centre Mark +

Hole

Slot

Slot

Bat Body

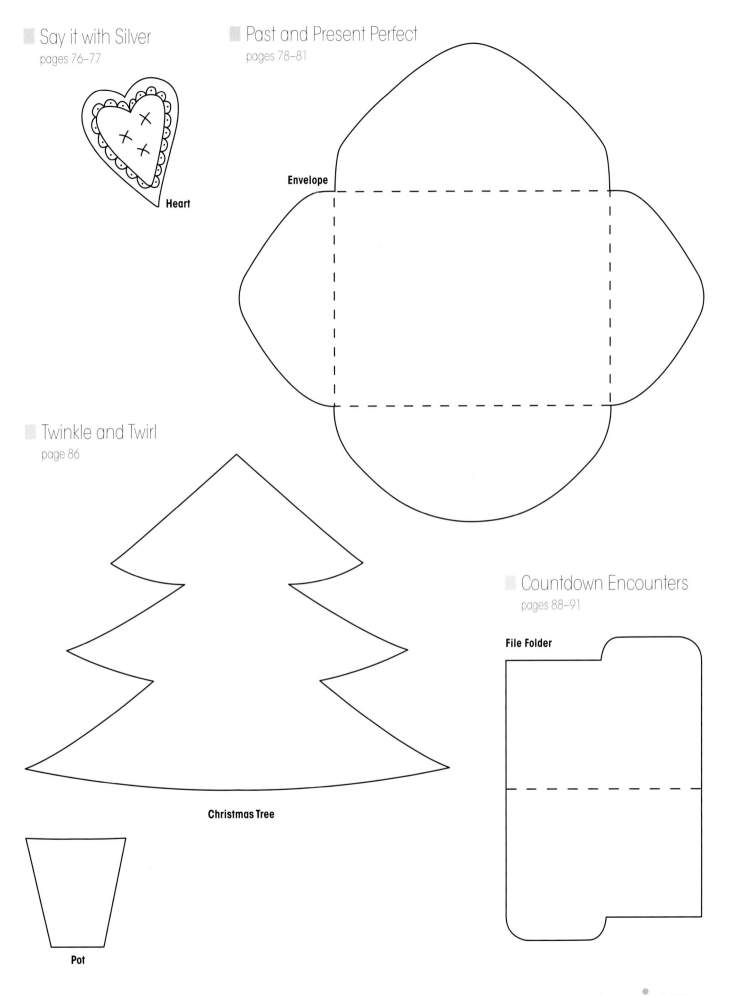

Say it with Silver
pages 76–77

Heart

Past and Present Perfect
pages 78–81

Envelope

Twinkle and Twirl
page 86

Christmas Tree

Pot

Countdown Encounters
pages 88–91

File Folder

Star Attraction
page 87

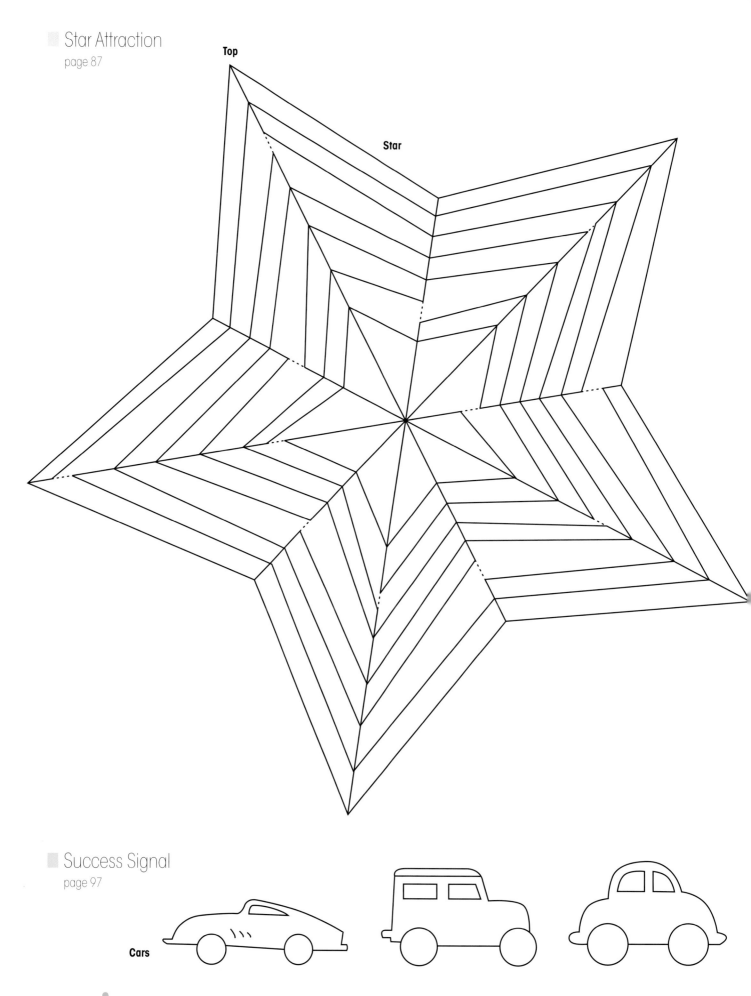

Top

Star

Success Signal
page 97

Cars

On The Move
page 93

Enlarge at 200%

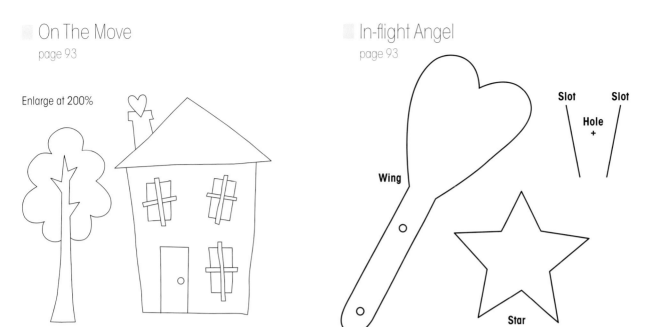

In-flight Angel
page 93

Slot Slot

Hole
+

Wing

Star

We Have Lift Off!
page 95

Fireworks

Flag

Hat

Slot

In the Frame
page 96

Heart

Strip

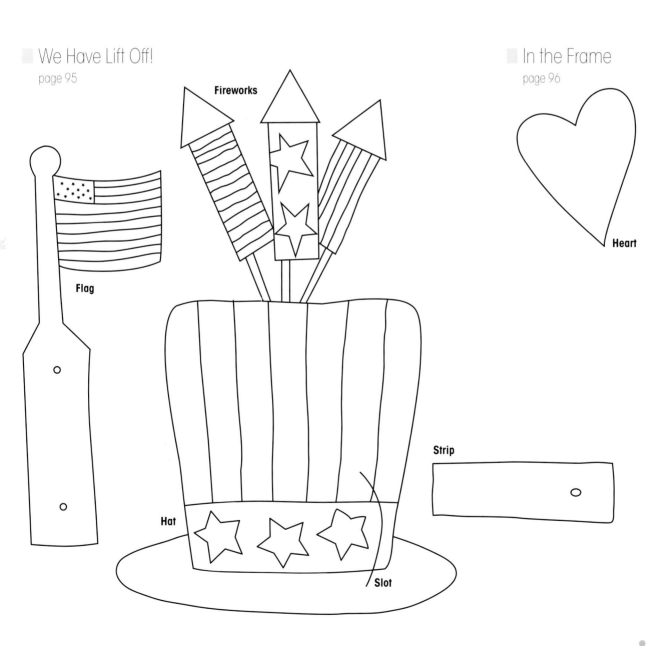

Suppliers

UK

Artbase
88 North Street, Hornchurch, Essex RM11 1SR
Tel: 01708 457 948 Email: artbasehx@aol.com
Website: www.artbasehornchurch.com

Bramwell Crafts *For nearest stockist:*
Old Empress Mills, Empress Street, Colne,
Lancashire BB8 9HU
Tel: 01282 860388 Email: info@bramwellcrafts.co.uk
Website: www.bramwellcrafts.co.uk

Capture the Magic
Staples Lodge, 15a Staples Lane, Soham,
Cambridgeshire CB7 5AF
Tel: 01353 720983
Email: vcarter@capturethemagic.biz
Website: www.capturethemagic.biz

Cotswold Keepsakes
The Parlour Workshop, Osney Hill Farm, North Leigh,
Witney, Oxfordshire OX29 6PJ
Tel: 01993 700246
Email: mail@cotswoldkeepsakes.co.uk
Website: www.cotswoldkeepsakes.co.uk

Craft Creations
Ingersoll House, Delamare Road, Cheshunt,
Hertfordshire EN8 9HD
Tel: 01992 781900
Email: enquiries@craftcreations.com
Website: www.craftcreations.com

Craftwork Cards
Unit 2, The Moorings, Waterside Road, Stourton,
Leeds LS10 1RW
Tel: 0113 276 5713 Email: info@craftworkcards.com
Website: www.craftworkcards.com

Hobbycraft
The Peel Centre, St Ann Way, Gloucester,
Gloucestershire GL1 5SF
Tel: 01452 424999 Website: www.hobbycraft.co.uk

Letraset
Kingsnorth Industrial Estate, Wotton Road,
Ashford, Kent TN23 6FL
Tel: 01233 624421 Email: info@letraset.com
Website: www.letraset.com

Memory Keepsakes
Shakeford Mill, Hinstock, Market Drayton, Shropshire TF9 2SP
Tel: 01630 638342
Email: sales@memorykeepsakes.co.uk
Website: www.memorykeepsakes.co.uk

Silver Lady Wedding Car Hire
The Old Rectory, 14 Netherby Road, Longtown, Carlisle CA6 5NT
Photographer – Malcolm Steels
Tel: 01228 792223
Email: enquiries@silverladyweddingcars.co.uk
Website: www.silverladyweddingcars.co.uk

Studio 8 Photography
8 Oxford Road, Kidlington, Oxfordshire OX5 1AA
Tel: 01865 842525 Email: info@studio-8.co.uk

Trimcraft
Mancor House, Bolsover Street, Hucknall
Nottingham NG15 7TZ
Website: www.trimcraft.co.uk

Whichcrafts?
29 Church Street, Barnoldswick, Lancashire BB18 5UR
Tel: 01282 851003 Email: crafts@whichcrafts.co.uk
Website: www.whichcrafts.co.uk

USA

Scrapbook Store
County Line Plaza, Tampa, Florida 33635
Tel: 813-814-5892
Email: info@scrapbookingsuppliesonline.com
Website: www.scrapbookingsuppliesonline.com

Scrapbook.com Superstore
116 N. Lindsay Rd, Suite 3, Mesa, Arizona 85213
Tel: 1–800-727272665
Email: store@scrapbook.com (for product queries)
Website: www.scrapbook.com

Stamping Bear
P O Box 52734, Durham, NC 27717
Email: mail@stampingbear.com
Website: www.stampingbear.com

Product Details

Fiskars products: available from Hobbycraft
Promarker™ pens (dual-tip marker pens), Safmat™ (self-adhesive clear printable film) and Studio Tac™ (dry adhesive tape): available from Letraset
Self-adhesive foil and Vivelle™: available from Craft Creations
Due to updating of products, the exact items listed may not be available at time of print, but do contact the suppliers for alternative designs.

An Amazing Arrival (pages 10–17)
Baby patterned papers, rubdowns and stickers and embellishments – Me and My Big Ideas, Soft Spoken range: available from Trimcraft

Mother's Day Magic (pages 18–25)
American Crafts, Sixth Avenue paper (patterned lightweight card): available from Craftwork Cards

Doodlebug Raspberry Sunrise Polka Dots paper; Doodlebug flower buttons (Bags of Love, pages 24–25); rickrack braid (Mum's Biggest Fan, pages 22–23): available from Capture the Magic

KI Memories Petite Pop paper (Bags of Love, pages 24–25): available from Cotswold Keepsakes

An Easter Extravaganza (pages 26–33)
Doodlebug Paradise Punch Polka Dots paper (patterned lightweight card): available from Capture the Magic

Father's Day Thrills (pages 34–41)
KI Memories, Favourite Things collection (Card with a Catch, pages 36–37, Best-dressed Bottle, pages 38–39); Karen Foster, Tan Fish Texture fish patterned paper (Card with a Catch, pages 36–37): available from Memory Keepsakes; Sapphire stardream paper (Best-dressed Bottle, pages 38–39, The Drive of his Life, pages 40–41): available from Cotswold Keepsakes

Wedding Wonders (pages 42–49)
Daisy D's Heritage, Heirloom and Music Collage papers; Making Memories metal embellishments: available from Cotswold Keepsakes; All Night Media 580K21 Music Score stamp, Personal Impressions P148N Champagne Glass stamp, Rubber Stampede 81424 Wedding Cake stamp, Hero Arts E3000 Hearts Leaves stamp (The Doorway to Our Future, pages 47–49): available from Whichcrafts?

Girl's Birthday Bliss (pages 50–57)
KI Memories, Friendship Palette large spotted patterned paper (Bags of Fun, pages 54–55); DCWV Cardstock Stack textured card (Flipbook Fashion, pages 56–57): available from Trimcraft

Halloween Horrors (pages 66–73)
Doodlebug Halloween patterned papers and stickers (Bat-mobile, pages 68–69, Spellbound, pages 70–72): available from Capture the Magic

Dress It Up Halloween buttons (Spellbound, pages 70–72, Party Pumpkin, page 73): available from Memory Keepsakes

Sensational Silver Wedding (pages 74–83)
Making Memories Cityscape Cardstock, Floral and Pinstripe in Spotlight: available from Trimcraft

Christmas Crackers (pages 84–91)
Doodlebug Christmas patterned papers, card stock, vellum and embellishments (Countdown Encounters, pages 88–91): available from Capture the Magic

Card Gallery (pages 92–97)
Art Accentz Flower Bradletz: available from Bramwell Crafts (On the Move, page 93)

Anita's Country Angel stamp: available from Hobbycraft; Cardmaker's Christmas Creative Pack: available from Trimcraft (In-flight Angel, page 93)

Doodlebug polka dots: available from Capture the Magic; baby patterned paper and square boat embellishment: available from Trimcraft (Calling Card, page 94)

Doodlebug papers and card: available from Capture the Magic; Hero Arts stitched flower stamps: available from Bramwell Crafts (Flowers in Depth, page 94)

Sizzlits Bounce die-cut alphabet: available from Capture the Magic; retirement stickers: available from Memory Keepsakes (Secret Pleasures, page 95)

One Heart… One Mind patterned lightweight card: available from Artbase (In the Frame, page 96)

Graduation hats patterned paper and stickers: available from Memory Keepsakes (Hats Off!, page 97)

Acknowledgments

It's been a pleasure putting this book together, but I wouldn't have been able to do it without friends who searched their photograph albums or took photographs of their children for some of the projects. The wedding pages would not look as stunning without the help of two professional photographers. Thanks to Clark Wiseman of Studio 8 for the gorgeous photo of the wedding couple and honeymoon car, and Malcolm Steels who took the photo of the white vintage Rolls Royce belonging to Silver Lady Wedding Cars. I must also thank Naomi Sisson, a young designer, for the fabulous teen girl pictures.

I'd like to thank Fiskars for supplying the paper trimmers, scissors and cutting mats, Trimcraft for lots of scrapbooking supplies and embellishments, Craft Creations for the scrapbook album and a variety of papers and card, as well as Letraset for craft knives, Promarker™ pens and Safmat™.

The editorial team at David and Charles have been excellent as usual – thanks to Cheryl, Prudence, Jennifer and Jo for their expertise and hard work. Thanks also to Simon Whitmore, who, once again, has taken some fantastic photographs. Finally, thanks to Ali Sharland, who allowed us to take over her house in Stroud for a few days for the finished photography.

Index